CONTENTS

how2become

JOIN THE ARMY
The Insider's Guide

HODDER
EDUCATION
AN HACHETTE UK COMPANY

Orders: Please contact Bookpoint Ltd, 130 Milton Park, Abingdon, Oxon
OX14 4SB. Telephone: (44) 01235 827720, Fax: (44) 01235 400454. Lines
are open from 9.00 to 5.00, Monday to Saturday, with a 24-hour message
answering service. You can also order through our website
www.hoddereducation.co.uk

British Library Cataloguing in Publication Data
A catalogue record for this title is available from the British Library.

ISBN: 978 1444 110586

First published   2010
Impression number 10 9 8 7 6 5 4 3 2 1
Year   2015 2014 2013 2012 2011 2010

Copyright © 2010 how2become Ltd

Cover image © Oleg_Zabielin – Fotolia.com

Typeset by Servis Filmsetting Ltd, Stockport, Cheshire
Printed in Great Britain for Hodder Education, An Hachette UK Company,
338 Euston Road, London NW1 3BH by Cox & Wyman Ltd, Reading,
Berkshire.

Hachette UK's policy is to use papers that are natural, renewable and
recyclable products and made from wood grown in sustainable forests.
The logging and manufacturing processes are expected to conform to the
environmental regulations of the country of origin.

INTRODUCTION

Welcome to *how2become: Join the Army: The Insider's Guide*. This guide has been designed to help you prepare for, and pass the British Army selection process.

The author of this guide, Richard McMunn, has spent more than 20 years in both the Armed Forces and the Emergency Services. He has vast experience and knowledge in the area of Armed Forces' recruitment and you will find his guidance both inspiring and highly informative. During his highly successful career in the Fire Service, Richard sat on many interview panels assessing candidates for selection. He has also been extremely successful at passing job interviews himself with a success rate of over 90 per cent! Follow his advice and preparation techniques carefully and you too can achieve the same levels of success in your career.

While the selection process for joining the Army is highly competitive, there are a number of things you can do in order to improve your chances of success, and they are all contained within this guide.

The guide itself has been divided into useful sections to make it easier for you to prepare for each stage. Read each section carefully and take notes as you progress. Don't ever give up on your dreams; if you really want to join the Army then you *can* do it. The way to prepare for a job in the Armed Forces is to embark on a programme of 'in depth' preparation, and this guide will show you exactly how to do that.

If you need any further help with the BARB test, getting fit or Army interview help and advice, then we offer a wide range of products to assist you. These are all available through our online shop www.how2become.co.uk.

Once again thank you for your custom and we wish you every success in your pursuit of a career in the Army.

Work hard, stay focused and be what you want . . .

Best wishes

The how2become team

The how2become Team

PREFACE

by author Richard McMunn

I can remember sitting in the Armed Forces careers office in Preston, Lancashire at the age of 16 waiting patiently to see the Warrant Officer who would interview me as part of my application for joining the Royal Navy. I had already passed the written tests, and despite never having sat an interview before in my life, I was confident of success.

In the build-up to the interview I had worked very hard studying all aspects of the job that I was applying for, and also perfecting my interview technique. At the end of the interview I was told that I had passed easily and all that was left to complete was the medical. Unfortunately I was overweight at the time and I was worried that I might fail because of that. At the medical my fears became a reality and I was told by the doctor that I would have to lose a stone in weight before the Army would accept me. I walked out of the doctor's surgery and began the walk to the bus stop to catch a bus that would take me back home three miles away. I was absolutely gutted, and embarrassed, that I had failed at the final hurdle, all because I was overweight!

I sat at the bus stop feeling sorry for myself and wondering what job I was going to apply for next. My dream of joining the Armed Forces was over and I didn't know which way to turn. Suddenly, I began to feel a sense of determination to lose the weight and get fit in the shortest time possible. It was at that particular point in my life when things began to change forever. As the bus approached I remember thinking there was no time like the present for getting started on my fitness regime. I therefore opted to walk the three miles home instead of being lazy and getting the bus. When I got home I sat in my room and wrote out a 'plan of action' that would dictate how I was going to lose the required weight. That plan of action was very simple, stating the following three things:

1. Every weekday morning I will get up at 6a.m. and run three miles.

2. Instead of catching the bus to college and then back home again I will walk.

3. I will eat healthily and I will not go over the recommended daily calorific intake.

Every day I would read my simple 'action plan' and it acted as a reminder of what I needed to do. Within a few weeks of following my plan rigidly I had lost over a stone in weight and I was a lot fitter too!

When I returned to the doctor's surgery for my medical the doctor was amazed that I had managed to lose the weight in such a short space of time and he was pleased that I had been so determined to pass the medical. Six months later I started my basic training course with the Royal Navy.

Ever since then I have always made sure that I prepare properly for any job application. If I do fail a particular interview or section of an application process then I will always go out of my way to ask for feedback so that I can improve for next time. I also still use an 'action plan' in just about every element of my work. Action plans allow you to focus your

mind on what you want to achieve and I will be teaching you how to use them to great effect in this book.

Throughout my career I have always been successful. It's not because I am better than the next person, but simply because I prepare better. I didn't do well at school so I have to work a lot harder to pass the exams and written tests that form part of a job application process, but I am always aware of what I need to do and what I must improve on.

I have always been a great believer in preparation. Preparation was my key to success, and it is also yours. Without the right level of preparation you will be setting out on the route to failure. The Armed Forces is hard to join, but if you follow the steps within this book then you will increase your chances of success dramatically.

Remember, you are learning how to be a successful candidate, not a successful soldier – that will come later.

The men and women of the Armed Forces carry out an amazing job. They are there to protect us and our country and they do that job with great pride, passion and very high levels of professionalism and commitment. They are to be congratulated for the job that they do.

Before you apply to join the Army you need to be fully confident that you too are capable of providing that same level of commitment. If you think you can do it, and you can rise to the challenge, then you just might be the type of person the Army is looking for. The Army's motto is 'Be the Best', and that's exactly what you should be aiming for during your preparation.

As you progress through this book you will notice that the qualities required to join the Army follow a common theme. You must learn to develop these qualities, and also be able to demonstrate throughout the selection process that you can meet them, if you are to have any chance of successfully passing the selection process.

CHAPTER I

HOW TO PASS THE ARMY SELECTION PROCESS

A career with the British Army is both rewarding and satisfying. Nowadays jobs for younger people are becoming increasingly harder to obtain, simply because employers are starting to look for people with more experience. The great thing about a career in the Army is that it will give you plenty of experience and make you very attractive to the majority of employers when you do eventually decide to leave after serving your contract. You will have the opportunity to gain many skills and qualifications during your time in the Armed Forces and you will also meet a large number of people who will become close friends and colleagues. Even though I left the Royal Navy 17 years ago I still keep in touch with a number of my old friends and colleagues.

Many young men and women apply to join the Army each year and a large number of them fail to pass the application process. In the majority of cases the people who failed could have avoided this by doing one thing – preparing effectively.

Try to imagine yourself as a soldier getting ready to go into battle or preparing to carry out a difficult reconnaissance mission. You've been briefed by your Commanding Officer, and he or she has told you what they expect. What would your next step be? Obviously you would begin to prepare for your mission and ensure that you carry it out to the best of your ability. However, your ability to prepare should start well before your Army career commences.

Why do we go to school? The answer is to prepare for life in society and hopefully to gain a number of qualifications that will allow us to become a good employee or even a competent self-employed person. Regardless of what grades you achieved at school, you must still prepare yourself fully for the Army selection process.

During your preparation it is important to remember that the smallest things can make the biggest difference. Try to imagine yourself as an Army Careers Officer. What would you be looking for in potential applicants? You would most probably be looking for a smart appearance, good personal hygiene, clean shoes, confidence, intelligence, manners and politeness to name but a few. An ability to listen to what you are being told is also very important and if you are asked to attend an interview or test at a specific time, then you must make sure you are punctual.

When I applied to join the Armed Forces many years ago I always attended the careers office in a suit, shirt and tie. Nobody had told me to do this but I wanted to stand out from the rest of the applicants and create the right impression. Your attitude is very important when you apply to join the Army and I will be teaching you how to demonstrate the right level of commitment and motivation throughout this book. In addition to reading this book it is crucial that you read thoroughly all of the recruitment literature that you are provided with, as you will certainly be asked questions on the information that is contained within it during the selection process. I would also strongly recommend that you obtain a

copy of *The British Army: A Pocket Guide*. This is a fantastic resource that will teach you all about the Army, its regiments and its equipment. You can get a copy of the book from www. how2become.co.uk.

Before we get cracking with how to pass the Army selection process I want you to promise yourself two things – the first is that you won't give up on your goal of joining the Army until you succeed and the second is that you will take positive steps to improve on your weak areas. Never give up on anything you do in life and make the word 'persevere' one of your favourite words. I love the word 'persevere', because if I do, then I know that it will lead me to success. You can't buy perseverance, but you can learn to implement it in everything that you do.

Learning Army values

This first step when preparing for any job is to learn and understand what the organisation you are applying to join expects of its employees. The same rule applies to the British Army.

As you can imagine the Army has a set of 'values' which everyone who works for it must follow and abide by. During the selection process, and in particular the interview, there is a strong chance that you will be asked to explain what the values are and what you understand about them. If I was to ask you the question 'Tell me what the British Army values are?' would you be able to answer it? If not then it is important that you learn them, but more importantly understand them. As a soldier you will often be required to do things that other people wouldn't want to do, or would be incapable of doing. As a soldier you will be highly trained and you will be able to carry out your tasks both professionally and competently. However, if the Army did not have these values and it did not have control of its people then things could soon go wrong. As a soldier it can be a difficult task balancing the aggression of combat with the self-discipline that is required to perform under immense pressure.

Let's now take a look at the values and what they mean.

The values of the British Army are as follows:

- **Selfless commitment** – putting other people before yourself.
- **Courage** – facing up to danger and doing what is right at all times.
- **Discipline** – being able to maintain constant high standards, so that others can rely on you.
- **Integrity** – earning the respect and trust of your work colleagues.
- **Loyalty** – being faithful to your work colleagues and to your duty.
- **Respect for others** – treating others with decency and respect at all times.

Before I go into more detail about each individual value I would recommend that you write each one of them down on a small piece of card or paper and carry it around with you in your wallet or purse. When you get a few spare minutes each day get the card out and read the values. They will soon become second nature to you and you will be able to reel them off quickly.

Selfless commitment

Every member of the Armed Forces must be totally committed. After all, it is the soldiers and officers who are the foundation of the British Army. You will need to perform to the best of your abilities at all times and you will be required to serve whenever and wherever the Army dictates. Putting the needs of the mission and your team ahead of your own needs is crucial at all times.

Courage

Soldiers are required to go into combat, and that takes unbelievable courage and commitment. Courage creates the

strength on which fighting spirit depends. Not only will you need the physical courage that is required but also mental courage. Even if the task or mission is highly dangerous you will need the strength of character and courage to always do what is right.

Discipline

In order for the Army to perform to the highest of standards then it needs its soldiers and officers to be disciplined. If they are not, then inevitably things will go wrong. Therefore you must obey all lawful orders that are given to you. Probably the most effective form of discipline is that of self-discipline. If you are self-disciplined then your life in the Army will be far easier. Self-discipline brings results and it also brings respect from colleagues and comrades. Without self-discipline you will soon land yourself in trouble and become more of a hindrance to your regiment than an asset. Self-discipline applies at all times whether you are on operations or not. You will also need self-discipline when you are off duty or on leave. When you join the Army you will become a respected member of society and people will look up to you. In essence you will become a role model for others, and that carries a lot of responsibility. You can't go brawling in the pub or getting yourself on the wrong side of the law. Throughout your Army career you should always look to set a good example.

Integrity

In order to reach the required level of integrity you will need to be trustworthy, honest, reliable, self-disciplined and sincere. Integrity is an essential part of Army life and unless you develop and maintain it then people will not trust you. If people do not trust you then the team fails – it's as simple as that.

Loyalty

When I left the Fire Service after 16 years' service I received a certificate from the Chief Fire Officer congratulating me on

my 'loyal and devoted service'. Those few words meant a tremendous amount to me as I know that I was totally loyal and devoted to the service throughout my time served. The Army is very similar to the Fire Service in that it requires its men and women to be loyal if it is to achieve its aim of working to the highest standards possible. As you can imagine, the nation and the Army rely on your commitment and support. You must be loyal to your commanders and to your work colleagues and also to your duty. Naturally you will not want to let your team down.

Respect for others

Having respect for others doesn't just form part of Army life – it also forms part of life in general. During the Army interviews that you will undergo during selection you will be asked questions that relate to your 'respect for people in positions of authority'. This could be your teachers at school or college or even local Police Officers. Let me ask you the question now: 'What do you think about your teachers at school?' Hopefully your answer will be that you have the highest level of respect for them. Unfortunately many young people do not have the maturity to respect people in positions of authority and this can lead to a failure in discipline. Before you apply to join the Army you must develop a respect for people in positions of authority, and to people in general. No form of bullying, harassment or discrimination will ever be tolerated in the Army and you must be able to treat people with dignity and respect. If only everybody in society treated everyone with respect then the world would be a much nicer place.

As a soldier you have the exceptional responsibility of using weapons and operating expensive equipment and machinery. In addition, you will sometimes have to live and work under extremely difficult conditions. In such circumstances, it is very important that you show the greatest respect for others. Effective teamwork, comradeship and leadership depend on respect and mutual trust.

Understanding the standards of conduct

In addition to the values of the British Army it is also important to be aware of the standards of conduct that you will be expected to abide by. Whilst it is not essential to learn these verbatim, it is a good idea to read them and be aware that they do exist. Throughout your career in the Army you will be required to follow strict discipline regulations. Anyone who breaks the rules or who acts in a manner which is damaging to the reputation of the Army may be subject to an investigation and possibly discipline procedures.

As a soldier serving in the British Army you must:

- Abide by the civil law, wherever you are serving.

- Abide by military law, which includes some additional offences such as insubordination and absence without leave, which are needed to maintain discipline.

- Abide by the laws of armed conflict whenever you are on operations.

- Avoid any activity that undermines your professional ability or puts others at risk, in particular, the misuse of drugs and abuse of alcohol.

- Avoid any behaviour that damages trust and respect between you and others in your team and unit, such as deceit or social misconduct. In particular, you must not commit any form of harassment, bullying or discrimination – whether on grounds of race, gender, religion or sexual orientation – or any other behaviour that could undermine good order and military discipline.

Now that we have taken a brief look at the values and the code of conduct that you will be expected to operate within it is time to explore the selection process.

CHAPTER 2
THE ARMY SELECTION PROCESS

The Army selection process is designed to test your suitability to life within the Army. It can be a difficult process if you don't prepare and can be a nerve-wracking one too. But the rewards of a career with the British Army are exceptional. A good salary, the chance to travel and to work as part of one of the most professional and respected organisations in the world make it all worthwhile. Whether you decide to pursue a career in IT/Communications, Healthcare, Logistics, Combat or Engineering, you can be certain that your career in the British Army will be rewarding and immensely satisfying.

In this chapter I have provided you with brief details relating to the selection process within the British Army. Later on I will go into more depth about each particular stage and how you can pass it. Remember that throughout the whole selection process the Army will be assessing you, so make sure you create a positive impression at all times. When you make your initial contact, either via the internet or by contacting/ visiting the Armed Forces Careers Office, remember that you

are under no obligation to join at this stage. Whilst the Army will not push you into joining it is still easy to get carried away with the prospect of joining such a service. It is important that you take your time to go away and thoroughly read the recruitment literature before making any decisions which will affect your life. Ask as many questions as you feel necessary so that you are fully aware of the commitment that you will be making. Remember to discuss your options with your parents and your partner to see how they feel. It is important that you have their support.

The Army selection process for a regular soldier consists of the following:

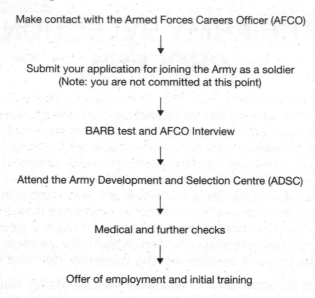

Make contact with the Armed Forces Careers Officer (AFCO)

⬇

Submit your application for joining the Army as a soldier
(Note: you are not committed at this point)

⬇

BARB test and AFCO Interview

⬇

Attend the Army Development and Selection Centre (ADSC)

⬇

Medical and further checks

⬇

Offer of employment and initial training

Make contact with the Armed Forces Careers Office (AFCO)

The first step in your pursuit to becoming a British Army soldier is to contact your local careers office. When you telephone the careers office you will need to inform it that you are interested

in a career with the British Army. It is perfectly acceptable not to have a career choice at this stage as you may not yet have access to any Army careers recruitment literature. Remember to be polite and courteous at all times when you speak to the Careers Officer. He or she may ask you a number of initial questions relating to whether or not you have any criminal convictions or whether you have had asthma at any time during your life. It is important that you are honest at every stage of the process; if you are not and this is discovered later it may jeopardise your chances of an Army career.

Make sure you have a pen, paper and your diary with you when you make your initial telephone call as you may be invited to attend for an initial chat at the Careers Office. Make a note of any meeting dates and ask questions if you are unsure of parking or directions, etc. Alternatively you may be sent an information pack to read and digest. When you receive the information pack, read it thoroughly.

Your initial meeting with the Army Careers adviser is as important as any other and remember that first impressions count for everything. Don't be late for your appointment and it is worthwhile checking the route to the AFCO prior to any scheduled meeting. If you are travelling by car ensure you know where to park and if you are taking public transport check train/ bus times as these can be unreliable. It is also worth taking a note of the Careers Office telephone number just in case you break down or anticipate being late. They will appreciate a courtesy call from you and in the majority of circumstances will be able to reschedule your meeting date if you have to cancel.

The night before your initial meeting get all of your clothes ironed and ready. The last thing you want on the morning of your meeting is to be rushing round looking for an ironed shirt, your shoes or tie, and this all forms part of your preparation for being successful.

When you arrive at the Careers Office introduce yourself in a polite manner and wait to be asked to be seated. These are all little tips that will help you to create the right impression.

Once you have obtained any relevant Army literature, had an initial discussion with the Careers Adviser and submitted your application form, you may be invited back to sit the British Army Recruit Battery test or BARB test as it is more commonly known.

Sit the BARB test

The BARB test is a computer screen selection test that assesses your ability to carry out tasks quickly and accurately. Although the test is usually conducted on a computer you should not have to use a keyboard, so if you are concerned about your computer skills then please don't be. The main purpose of the BARB test is to assess which jobs you are most suited to. Therefore it is important that you obtain high scores. Basically, the higher your scores the more career options you will have.

The computer version of the test requires you to input 'touch screen' answers after following simple instructions. There are approximately five sections to the test and I have provided you with lots of sample practice questions in a later chapter. Make sure you work through the questions thoroughly, and under timed conditions. I will provide you with plenty of advice and assistance later on in relation to this test so don't panic if you aren't very good at this form of testing. The Army will also provide you with a BARB test booklet before you attend the real assessment. This booklet again will provide you with some practice questions and it is important that you complete all of the questions provided. The Army requires you to take the completed booklet with you to the test centre, so make sure you don't forget it. When you are working through the BARB booklet at home take your time to make sure you answer the questions correctly; this also ensures that you understand what is required of you when you sit the real test. Remember to practise the sample test questions that are contained within the 'BARB test' section of this book.

Once you have completed the BARB test your AFCO careers adviser will sit down with you and discuss your scores in

detail. He or she will also ask you questions relating to your fitness levels, the reasons why you want to join the Army, and the preparation you have undertaken so far. The adviser will then inform you what career options are available to you based on your results and whether or not you are going to be put forward to the Army Development and Selection Centre.

Attend the Army Development and Selection Centre

If you are successful at the BARB test stage and you are put forward for recommendation by your AFCO adviser, then you will be asked to attend the Army Development and Selection Centre (ADSC) for two days. ADSCs are sited at various UK locations such as Lichfield, Pirbright, Glencorse in Scotland and Ballymena in Northern Ireland.

Candidates who attend the ADSC will be required to stay overnight. During the two-day ADSC assessment each candidate will undergo the following:

- a thorough medical examination

- an ice breaker where each candidate must give a 2 minute introductory presentation to the rest of the group

- physical assessment tests which include sit-ups, press-ups, pull-ups (heaves), static dynamic weight lift, back extension test, gym tests, jerry can carry and a 2.4 km (1.5-mile) best effort run: there will also be some team relay exercises which are held in the evening

- a technical selection test (only applicable to those who are applying for technical trades)

- team building tasks, to assess the ability of the candidates to work in a team and any leadership potential they may have

- an interview with an Army Development and Selection Officer (ADSO).

During your stay at the ADSC you will get to see the type of training that you will undergo if successful, and you will also have the opportunity to talk to recruits who are already in training.

After the final interview with the Army Development Selection Officer you will then be informed if you have been successful, and if so, offered a vacancy in a particular trade and regiment or corps.

Selecting the right Army career

Before you apply to join the Army you will need to decide what career you want. This can easily be achieved by visiting the Army website at www.armyjobs.mod.uk and using the job explorer tool. This is an extremely useful tool that will allow you to select the right job for you based on certain criteria including type of position and time commitment. Of course, you will only be permitted to apply for your chosen career if you reach the required standard during selection, which includes BARB test results and the successful completion of the ADSC assessment.

It is crucial that you make the right career choice from the offset and your Armed Forces Careers Office adviser will be best placed to provide advice and guidance in this area. Once you have thoroughly read your recruitment literature and visited the Army website to make your career choice(s) then you can begin to prepare for a successful application.

CHAPTER 3
THE TOP TEN INSIDER TIPS FOR SUCCESS

Over the next few pages I will provide you with ten very important tips. The majority of these tips will appear to be obvious but the vast amount of applicants who apply to join the Army will not focus on any of them. If you follow each one of them carefully and integrate them as a part of your preparation strategy then your chances of success will greatly increase. Do not settle for average scores during the selection but instead aim for excellence as this will stand you in good stead for your entire career. Learn good habits now and the rest will follow.

1 Be fully prepared and focused, and learn how to use 'action plans' to ensure continuous improvement

In order to become a British Army Soldier you will need to be fully prepared and focused. As with any selection process for any job or career you need to prepare yourself fully. You should carry out as much research as possible about the Army and your chosen career or trade. When you decide to

apply to join the Army you need to understand what the job is about and how it will affect your life, both professionally and socially. The British Army is looking for people who are professional, flexible, committed and motivated along with being an effective team player.

You will be required to sit a number of tests and exercises throughout the selection process, including tests that assess your physical fitness. Again, you must prepare for every eventuality. The Army will require you to run a set distance (1.5-miles) within a set time and the only way to prepare for this is to practise, practise and practise some more! You will recall at the start of this book that I always use an action plan in everything that I do which is work related. An action plan will focus your mind on the task that lies ahead of you. If I was applying to join the Army today then I would most probably use a weekly timetable of preparation that looks something like this:

Monday	Tuesday	Wednesday	Thursday	Friday	Saturday	Sunday
30 minutes BARB Test preparation and 30 minutes Technical Selection Test preparation	60 minutes study relating to my choice of career	60 minutes psychometric test preparation	Rest day	60 minute study relating to Army life, equipment and weapons	30 minute BARB Test preparation and 30 minute Technical Selection Test preparation	30 minutes study relating to my choice of career

Monday	Tuesday	Wednesday	Thursday	Friday	Saturday	Sunday
30 minute run	45 minutes gym work (light weights)	30 minute run or bleep test preparation	Rest day	1.5-mile run (best effort) and bleep test preparation	Rest day	Rest day

The above timetable would ensure that I focused on the following three key development areas:

1. improving my mental and physical fitness

2. improving my ability to carry out psychometric tests

3. improving my knowledge of the Army and my chosen career.

You will also need to work on your interview technique and responses to the questions but that comes later in the book.

The point to stress is that if you have some form of structure to your preparation then you are far more likely to succeed. Remember that one of the assessable areas during selection is 'reaction to regiment and routine'. By following a structured training and development programme during your preparation you are experiencing some form of positive routine in your life.

2 Practise lots of BARB test and psychometric test questions

When you apply to join the Army you will be required to sit what is known as the British Army Recruit Battery Test (BARB), which I have already mentioned. This is designed to test your ability to quickly and accurately carry out set tasks that are presented before you. Most applicants to the British Army will not prepare themselves for this test, and although they

may achieve the required pass mark they will only be offered a number of careers and may not get the one that they really want. By improving your scores on the BARB test you can increase the number of career options available to you. The only really effective way to improve your scores on the day of the test is to carry out plenty of sample test questions, under timed conditions, in the build up to the test. In addition to the BARB test you will also be required to sit a literacy test as part of the Army Development and Selection Centre (ADSC) process. For those candidates who are applying for technical trades such as the Royal Engineers, you will also be required to sit a Technical Selection Test. The most effective way to prepare for this type of test is to obtain a GCSE level Maths testing booklet.

Within this book I have provided you with lots of sample test questions to help you prepare for the BARB test. Make sure you integrate lots of sample test question work into your preparation strategy. Practise these tests little and often. Thirty minutes' practice every other day will be far more effective than five hours the night before your test.

3 Be polite and courteous at all times, try your hardest and have the right attitude

Common courtesy and good manners are often lacking in society today. You must remember that you are trying to join a disciplined service which requires you to act in a particular manner. When you apply to join the British Army you will be communicating at times with experienced and professional officers. They are highly trained to pick out those people who they believe are worthwhile investing time and money in, and they will be assessing you right from the word go.

When you telephone the Armed Forces Careers Office, either to obtain an application form or arrange an informal chat, be polite and courteous at all times. General good manners such as 'good morning', 'good afternoon', 'thank you for your time' and 'please' are not as commonplace in today's

society as they used to be. Being polite and courteous when communicating with the Army Careers Officer can help you to create the right impression from the start.

During my time in the Fire Service I interviewed scores of people wanting to join and it was those people who were polite, respectful and courteous who grabbed my attention. First impressions are very important and if you can demonstrate a level of self-discipline before you join then this will work in your favour.

Going the extra mile to make a good impression will work wonders, and it will help you to create a positive rapport with the Recruitment Officer. When you attend the Army Development and Selection Centre (ADSC) you will be assessed right from the start. Whilst at the ADSC do not put your hands in your pockets or cross your arms, and make sure you stand tall at all times. Don't give any 'back chat' to the ADSC staff and leave the bad attitude behind. See the section on preparing for the ADSC process for more tips and advice.

4 Choose the right career

During the initial stages of the selection process you will be asked to select up to three career options in order of priority. Make sure you research the careers available by studying the literature the Army provides you with when you register your interest. Don't just look at the glamorous pages but read fully what each job entails. Remember that an Army career can be a long one and you need to aim for the career that is best suited to you and your circumstances. Be sensible and thoroughly research the careers available before making your selection.

There are seven different job categories in the Army including logistics and support, combat, engineering, intelligence, IT and communications, music and ceremonial, human resources and medical. Every single person who works in the Army has a role to play, which makes for a highly effective

team operation. By reading all of the literature fully you will also be preparing yourself better for the selection process. What if you are asked the following question during your interview? Could you answer it?

'Tell me what your chosen career involves?'

Imagine if you've only looked at the pictures and you don't know what that particular job entails! It won't look good and it also demonstrates that you have not prepared yourself fully. You will have noticed that within the timetable I provided in tip 1 I dedicated plenty of time each week to studying my chosen career. During the selection process you will be asked questions about your chosen career, what it involves, the training and the reasons why you have chosen it.

5 Be smart and well turned out

There's an old saying: 'shiny shoes, shiny mind'. How many people do you know who clean their shoes every day? Not many I'm sure, but this can go a long way towards creating the right impression and getting you into the right frame of mind for Army life. When I was preparing for my career in the Armed Forces my father taught me how to use an iron and how to clean my shoes correctly. I can remember him showing me how to iron a shirt and a pair of trousers, and initially I thought it was waste of time. However, when I joined the forces this training my father had given me proved to be invaluable. Not only did it provide me with some routine and discipline but it also forced me to take a pride in my appearance – something which is crucial to your role as a British Army soldier.

Walking into the careers office with dirty shoes doesn't create a good impression. As a British Army soldier you will be inspected every day on your turnout and it is far better to demonstrate to the Careers Officer that you have the ability to be smart before you begin your basic training. Your budget

might not be large, but you can purchase an inexpensive shirt and tie or smart blouse. They don't have to be of expensive quality but by showing that you've made an effort you will again create the right impression. If you cannot afford to buy these items then you may be able to borrow from a friend or relative.

It is definitely worth investing time and effort on your appearance as wearing jeans, t-shirt and trainers when attending the careers office or the ADSC is not going to create the right impression.

Tips for creating the right impression

- Dress smartly every time you attend the Careers Office and also when you attend the ADSC.

- Make sure your shoes are cleaned and polished at all times. Get into the habit of polishing your shoes every day.

- Don't wear bright coloured socks with your suit!

- Learn how to wear a tie correctly.

---

6 Understand the Army selection process scoring criteria

During the Army selection process you will be assessed against a number of set criteria. Amongst others, the scoring criteria include areas such as knowledge of the Army, motivation, your determination to succeed and your experience of being self-reliant. If you understand what the Army is looking for from its potential recruits then you have a higher chance of succeeding. Take a look at the next section, 'The Army scoring criteria', for some useful hints and advice on how to improve your scores during the selection process. Once you have read this section, write down on a blank sheet of paper the areas that you think

you need to improve on, and then take action. For example, if you find that your knowledge of Army life is limited then start to read the recruitment literature and visit the Army websites in order to gain a better understanding of what the service involves.

Do everything in your power to improve your chances of success.

7 Get fit for service

Before you apply to join the British Army as a soldier you should be physically active and fit. It is essential that you can easily pass the physical tests. Within this book I have provided you with a free 'How to get Army fit' guide, which has been designed to assist you in your preparation. One of the best ways to improve your physical fitness is to go running. Just by running 3 miles, three times a week you will be amazed at how much your fitness and general well-being will improve. You will begin to feel better about yourself and your scores on the BARB test are likely to improve too as your concentration levels will be far better.

During the ADSC assessment you will be required to run 1.5-miles in your fastest time possible. Again, as part of my timetable in tip 1 I included a number of runs and gym sessions which are designed to assist my physical fitness and strength. I also included a 1.5-mile run test and I would try to improve on this time each week. Keep trying to improve yourself and remember – be the best that you can.

I'd also recommend that you obtain a copy of the multi-stage fitness test or bleep test as it is otherwise called. You can usually download this test from the internet or purchase it through sites such as Amazon.co.uk. Make the effort to practise the bleep test at least twice a week and try to improve on your level each time you do it.

Tips for getting fit for selection

- Practise the bleep test at least twice a week. This will be excellent for increasing your cardiovascular fitness.

- Embark on a structured running programme that is aimed at achieving 1.5-miles in well under 14 minutes.

- Get down the gym and start working out with light weights including exercises that will increase your upper and lower body strength.

- Work on your Sit-ups and Press-ups, and be capable of doing at least 50 of each within a 2-minute period.

- Before you attend the ADSC assessment be able to do at least 10 pull-ups or heaves as they are otherwise called. If you don't have access to a gym then consider buying a pull-up bar that you can use at home. Make sure it conforms to the relevant safety standards. You don't want to incur an injury during your fitness preparation. There are different standards for different regiments in this test. For example, candidates who are applying for the Royal Engineers will require a greater level of upper body strength so therefore the required amount of pull-ups will be greater.

- Start running early in the morning – preferably at 6a.m.! This will get you used to the early starts. Don't forget to stretch properly before any form of exercise.

- Make sure your sports equipment is comfortable and it fits correctly.

8 Understand the word 'teamwork' and have experience of working in a team

The British Army prides itself on its great ability to operate as a team unit. Think of the best football teams in the country. Those that are the most successful are not the ones that

have one or two great players, but that have the best overall team. The ability to work as part of a team is essential, and you will be assessed on this throughout the selection process.

Within the Army you will be required to work in a team environment every day in order to carry out tasks both small and large. Whether you are working as an Aviation Support Specialist or a Chef, you will need to have very good team-working skills. Although team skills will be taught during your training, you will still need to demonstrate that you have the potential to become a competent team member throughout the selection process. It is far better if you have experience of working as part of a team prior to joining the Army. If you play a form of team sports then even better. There are many definitions of the word 'teamwork' but the one that I believe sums it up most effectively is:

'The process of working effectively with a group of people in order to achieve a goal.'

You may find in some work situations, either now or in the future, that there are people who you dislike for various reasons. It is your ability to work with these people during difficult circumstances that makes you a good and effective team member. It is also about your ability to listen to other people's ideas and involve them in the team decisions that sets you apart from the rest. Be a team player and not an individual who knows best!

Some of the qualities of a good team player include:

- the ability to listen to others' suggestions
- being able to communicate effectively
- being capable of solving problems
- coming up with a variety of solutions to a problem
- being hard working and focused on achieving the task
- being professional and doing a good job

- helping and supporting others

- being capable of listening to a brief and following clear instructions.

9 Prepare effectively for the interviews

During the selection process you will be required to sit a number of interviews designed to test your suitability to join the Army. The selection officers are looking for you to demonstrate the potential and ability to become a professional and competent British Army soldier. You will be required to sit interviews both at the Armed Forces Careers Office (AFCO) and also at the Army Development and Selection Centre (ADSC). I previously mentioned that first impressions are important, so during the interview you need to create the right impression, from the clothes that you wear to how you communicate and even down to how you sit in the interview chair.

Within this book I have dedicated an entire chapter to interviews and the information that I provide you with will be a great asset during your preparation. I would estimate that I have been successful in over 90 per cent of interviews I have attended during my career. The reason for that success is not because I am a special person but solely down to the amount of effort I put into my preparation. I always carry out a 'mock' interview' before I attend the real interview and this goes a long way to helping me to succeed.

Tips for passing the interviews

- Practise a 'mock' interview. Basically this entails asking a friend or relative to interview you under formal conditions. Get them to ask you all of the interview questions that are contained within this book and try answering them.

- Prepare your responses prior to the interview. This does not mean learning the answers to the interview questions

---

(Continued)

(Continued)

> 'parrot fashion', but instead having a good idea of how you intend to respond to them.
>
> • Concentrate on your interview technique. Sit upright in the interview chair, do not slouch, speak clearly and concisely, and address the panel members in an appropriate way, such as 'Sir' or 'Ma'am'.

10 Practise 'deliberately' and 'repetitively' to improve

This final tip is an outstanding one, and one that I strongly recommend you implement during your preparation for joining the Army.

History has proven that high-performing individuals have two things in common. This first is that they deliberately identify what it is they are weak at, and then they go full out to improve it. The second common factor is that they repeat their practice on their weak areas time and time again. Eventually they will become outstanding at what they do. Let me give you an example. David Beckham is an outstanding footballer. He is renowned for his highly accurate crossing of the ball and free kick taking. Now of course, David had a natural ability to play football from an early age but it wasn't this natural ability that made him so good at crossing the ball or taking free kicks. It was his 'deliberate' practice and the 'repetitive' nature of that practice that made him so good.

Before you go any further in this book I want you to think for a minute or two and write down the exact areas of the selection process that you believe you are weak in. Select your weak areas from the following list:

• 1.5-mile run

• sit-ups

• press-ups

- pull-ups
- the multi-stage fitness test (bleep test)
- the BARB test
- aptitude and literacy tests
- interview skills
- your knowledge of your chosen trade
- your knowledge of the Army and Army life
- your attitude.

Once you have decided on your weak areas you then need to implement a plan that involves lots of repetitive practice. The obvious downside to continuous and repetitive practice is that it is physically and mentally tiring. However, if you are committed to improving and reaching the peak of your abilities then the extra effort is certainly worthwhile.

Too many people give up at the first hurdle. If you realise that your fitness is not yet up to the required standard then take positive steps to improve it. If you find that your scores on the BARB test are not sufficient for the career you want, then go away and practise so that the next time you take it you succeed. We all have to come face to face with hurdles or setbacks during life but it is how we deal with them that is important. Don't view failure as final. Instead, view it as an opportunity for development.

Talk to the AFCO recruitment officer and ask him or her how you can improve your chances of success. Practise plenty of test questions and mock interviews, and get out there running in order to improve your fitness. I can assure you that if you pass the selection process through sheer determination and hard work you will feel a great sense of achievement that will stay with you for the rest of your life. Make success a habit.

CHAPTER 4
THE ARMY SCORING CRITERIA

In this chapter I will provide you with information that relates to how the Army will assess you during the selection process. Please note that the assessable criteria for the BARB test and some elements of the ADSC assessment are different. The criteria that I am going to provide you with during this chapter relates to your own personal attributes and qualities, and also your knowledge of the Army and your chosen career. This information will act as a very good foundation for your preparation. If you are capable of providing the Army selecting officers with what they are looking for then your chances of success will greatly increase.

The marking sheet used to assess your abilities covers a number of different assessable areas. The following list is a selection of some of the criteria used:

- personal turnout
- sociability
- emotional maturity and stability

- drive and determination to succeed
- physical robustness
- experience of being self-reliant
- reaction to social discipline
- experience of and reaction to regimentation and routine
- knowledge and experience of Army life
- motivation to join the Army
- personal circumstances.

This list is not exhaustive and there will be other areas that the Army will be assessing you on during the interviews and written tests. However, having an understanding of the qualities you need to demonstrate throughout selection will improve your chances of success dramatically.

Personal turnout

The Army is looking for you to be smartly dressed when you attend the Armed Forces Careers Office (AFCO), the ADSC assessment and during your interview. Interviewers also want to see that you have made an effort to present yourself positively. When you attend the careers office, whether it is for an interview or a careers presentation, always make sure you wear a formal outfit such as a suit or shirt and tie. Whilst this is not essential it will allow you to score higher in the area of 'personal turnout'.

Many people will stroll into the careers office wearing jeans and trainers. Make an effort to stand out for the right reasons and this will certainly work in your favour. Those people who turn up to the AFCO dressed untidily and unwashed or unshaven will score poorly. Throughout this book I will make reference to the importance of dressing smartly and making the effort to present yourself in a positive, motivated and professional manner.

Tips for scoring highly on personal turnout

- Make sure your shoes are clean and polished.

- Shirt, trousers and tie for males and a smart formal outfit for females are required.

- Ensure your clothes are clean, ironed and uncreased.

- Work on your personal hygiene and overall appearance. Make sure your nails are clean!

- Stand tall and be confident.

- Don't slouch in the interview chair.

Sociability

This section assesses your ability to mix well with people. The Army wants to know that you are socially confident and outgoing. It is also important that you have a good sense of humour. Interviewers want to know that you can fit in well with the Army way of life and that you have no problems with communal living.

When you join the Army you will be required to live in accommodation that houses many people. As you progress up through the ranks the amount of people that you'll be required to live with will decrease, until eventually you get a room on your own! Some people find it very difficult to socialise with others and these are not the ones the Army wants to recruit. Officers need people who will adopt the team spirit and who have no problems with communicating with others. Those applicants who come across as quiet or shy will not score well in the area of sociability. However, at no point during selection should you be brash, abrasive or a non-team player.

> ## Tips for scoring high in sociability
>
> - During the interviews provide examples of where you have mixed well with others. This may be through youth organisations such as the Scouts, etc.
>
> - If you have played team sports then this will be an advantage.
>
> - Tell the interviewer that you have no problem with communal living. (Communal living is living with other people.) You may be in a room of up to 30 other people whilst in your training, so interviewers want to know that you are comfortable with this.
>
> - Smile and laugh where appropriate – a sense of humour is a must but never be over-bearing or over-confident. Never 'back chat' or be disrespectful to the recruiting officers and staff.

Emotional maturity and stability

The Army want to see that you are mature for your age and that you are even tempered and well balanced. Officers don't want people who are aggressive or who come across with a bad attitude. They want to see that you have coped well with the ups and downs of life so far and you may find that they ask you questions on any difficult areas of life that you have had to deal with. They want to know that you will adapt well to the change in lifestyle when you join the Army and that you can cope in highly stressful situations. The Army will also be looking for you to be mature for your age and that there are no signs of depression or anxiety. Interviewers will also be assessing your ability to cope well with unfamiliar surroundings and that you will not become homesick during training.

Tips for scoring high in emotional maturity and stability

- During the interviews and during discussions with the Armed Forces Careers Office adviser try to provide examples of where you have dealt well with difficult situations in your life in a positive and mature manner.
- Try to be upbeat and positive about the future.
- Don't be over-confident or 'macho'.

Drive and determination to succeed

The Army wants to know that you have a sense of purpose in your life. Assessors will be looking for a pattern of achievement, either through school or at work, and for evidence that you are not easily deflected from your goals and aspirations. They want to see that you are a competitive person who is highly motivated to succeed. You will recall at the beginning of this book how much emphasis I put on perseverance. Drive and determination are very similar to perseverance in that you have the ability to keep working hard and improving yourself until you achieve success.

Those applicants who show signs that they give up easily or have no goal aspirations will score poorly in the area of drive and determination to succeed.

Tips for scoring high in drive and determination to succeed

- Provide examples of what you have achieved. This might be educational qualifications, courses that you have attended or sporting achievements.

(Continued)

(Continued)

- Be positive about joining the Army and tell interviewers that nothing is going to stop you from succeeding. If you don't pass this time then you will look for ways to improve the next time you apply.

- Demonstrate that your ambition and sense of purpose is to join the Army and become a professional and competent soldier.

Physical robustness

The Army wants to see that you engage in outdoor activities and that you have some experience of playing team sports. Being physically active is important and if you are strong and free from injuries and weakness then this will be an advantage during selection. If you are not involved in any form of team sports then I advise that you start straightaway. It is very easy to become involved in team sports as there are so many to choose from, for example netball, football, hockey, rugby and basketball.

Those applicants who provide evidence that they are isolated individuals who spend too much time at home on the computer or watching TV will score lower than those who are physically active.

Tips for scoring high in physical robustness

- Be involved in competitive team sports.

- Be an active, outdoor type person.

- Attend the gym and carry out light weight exercises and workouts.

Experience of being self-reliant

The Army wants to know that you can handle the pressure of living away from home. If you have travelled or have been on camps where you have had to 'rough it' then this is an advantage. Basically assessors want to know that you can look after yourself without the help of your parents or home comforts.

If you have no experience whatsoever of being self-reliant then take steps now to improve your experience in this area. For example, there is nothing to stop you from going camping for the weekend or joining the Army Cadets where you will be able to gain experience of this important attribute.

Tips for scoring high in being self-reliant

- Provide examples of where you have been away from home for short or long periods of time.

- Tell the interviewer that you enjoy travelling and being away from home. Remember that it is important to provide examples of when you did this and where.

- Tell the interviewer that you are looking forward to leaving home to join the Army and facing the challenges that it presents.

- Provide examples of where you have had to fend for yourself or where you have been away camping.

Reaction to social discipline

The Army wants to see that you have a positive attitude towards authority. People in authority include the police, your parents, teachers and even your boss at work. When you join the Army you will be taking orders from senior officers and they want to know that you have no problem with authority.

how2become

There is a strong possibility that the interviewer will ask you questions that relate to your attitude to education and your teachers. At no point should you be negative about your teachers or about people who are in positions of authority. If you are disrespectful or negative about these people then there is a strong possibility that the Army selection officers will take a dim view of your attitude. For example, I have come across applicants who complain during the Army interview that their teachers were rubbish at their job and that everyone in the class would always laugh at them. As you can imagine, those applicants do not progress any further during the selection process.

Tips for scoring high in social discipline

- Try to provide examples of when you have carried out orders, either at work or at school.

- Tell the interviewer that you respect authority – providing you do of course – and that you see it as an important aspect of life. You do not have a problem with taking orders from anyone, even those of the opposite sex.

Experience of and reaction to regimentation and routine

When you join the Army you will lose much of your personal freedom. During your initial training there will be many restrictions placed upon you in terms of leave and your general freedom. You won't be given the time to do all of the things that you usually do whilst at home. Therefore, the Army wants to see that you have the ability to cope with this additional pressure and disciplined routine.

You must try to demonstrate during the selection process that you have already experienced some form of routine and that you are capable of following rules and regulations. This could simply be by having some form of disciplined routine at

home, whereby you are required to clean the house and carry out the ironing for a few hours every week.

Tips for scoring high in experience of and reaction to regimentation and routine

- Provide examples of where you have lost your personal freedom, either during your upbringing, at school or during work. Maybe you have had to work unsociable hours or had to dedicate time and effort into your educational studies?

- Tell the interviewer that you fully understand that you will lose your personal freedom when you join the Army and that it won't be a problem for you.

- Implement some form of routine into your preparation strategy for joining the Army. Set out your action plan early on and follow it rigidly.

Knowledge and experience of Army life

Gaining knowledge of Army life can be achieved in a number of ways. If you have been a member of any youth organisations then this will be an obvious advantage. Youth organisations include the Scouts, Army Cadets, Air Training Corps or Sea Cadets, etc. If a member of your family or a friend is a member of the Armed Forces then you can also gain knowledge through them simply by asking them questions about their job and life within the Armed Forces. It is also important to gain knowledge of Army life by reading your recruitment literature and visiting the Army website if you have access to the internet.

Another fantastic way to gain invaluable knowledge of how the Army operates and its equipment is to get a copy of *The British Army: A Pocket Guide*. This book sells for approximately £5.99 and it fits easily into your pocket. Any spare moments

you have during the day you can start reading about vital facts that relate to the British Army.

Tips for scoring high in knowledge and experience of Army life

- Speak to any friends or relatives who are members of the Armed Forces and ask them what it is like. Gain as much information as possible from the AFCO staff and also through your recruitment literature.

- Find out as much as possible about the training you will undertake when you join the Army for your chosen career and also your initial recruit training.

- Consider visiting an Army establishment or museum. These are great places to learn about Army life.

- Consider joining a youth organisation such as the Scouts or Cadets to gain some experience of a disciplined service.

Motivation to join the Army

The Army wants to see that it is your decision to join and that you haven't been pushed into it by friends or family. Joining the Army to become a soldier first and learn a trade second is also important. Interviewers want to see that you have been pulled by the attractions of the Army as opposed to being pushed into them. If you are successful in your application the Army will be investing a tremendous amount of time, energy and money into your training and development. The last thing it wants is that you decide it's not for you. Once you join the Army you will have to serve 28 days in training. After the 28th day you can apply in writing to leave. If you're under 18 when you join, you have six months to let the Army know your decision and three months if you are over 18. Once this time has passed you are committed to serving

your contract so you must be 100 per cent certain that it's for you.

Tips for scoring high in motivation to join the Army

- Always present a positive attitude towards joining when you visit the AFCO and also whilst attending the ADSC. This choice of career should be something that you considered very carefully and you have been working very hard to make sure that you pass.

- Try to think about what attracts you to the Army and tell the interviewer during selection.

Personal circumstances

The Army will want to know that you have the support of your family and/or your partner. They also want to see that you are free from any detracting circumstances such as financial difficulties. If you are in financial difficulty then this could have a negative effect on your mental health during training. They will assess your personal circumstances during selection and also at the ADSC interview.

Tips for scoring high in personal circumstances

- Speak to your parents and your partner (if applicable) about your choice of career. Ask them for their support.

- If they do not support you or they are concerned about you joining then I would recommend that you take them along to the AFCO so that the Careers Officer can talk to them about Army life and answer any questions that they may have. It is imperative that you have their full support.

CHAPTER 5
THE AFCO AND ADSC INTERVIEWS

During the Army selection process you will be required to sit a number of interviews both at the Armed Forces Careers Office (AFCO) and at the Army Development and Assessment Centre (ADSC). The information that I have provided in this chapter will assist you during your preparation for both sets of interviews.

The Army will use a set marking sheet for your interviews and the questions will be based around a number of specific criteria. The questions will vary from interview to interview but the core elements are designed to assess whether you are suitable to join the service. The following is a list of areas you may be asked questions on during your Army interview and you need to use these as a basis for your preparation:

- the reasons why you want to join the Army

- the reasons why you have chosen your particular job, trade and regiment

- what information you already know about the Army, your chosen regiment and the lifestyle and training

- information about your hobbies and interests including sporting activities

- any personal responsibilities that you currently have at home, at school or at work.

- information about your family and what they think about you joining the Army: do they support you?

- information based around your initial application form

- your experience of work and education and whether or not you have had any responsibility at home or work

- your emotional stability and your maturity

- your drive and determination to succeed

- any experience you have of working as part of a team

- your attitude towards physical exercise and team sports

- your reaction to the disciplined environment

- your knowledge of life within the Army.

Over the next few pages I have provided you with a number of sample interview questions and responses. These will act as a good basis for your preparation. However, it is important to point out at this stage the responses you provide during the interview should be based solely on your own experiences and opinions.

Sample interview question I

Why do you want to join the Army?

This is an almost guaranteed question during your Army interview so there should be no reason why you can't answer it in a positive manner. Try to display motivation when answering questions of this nature. The Army is looking for people who want to become a professional member of its team and who understand the Army way of life. By studying your Army recruitment literature and the Army website you will understand what service life is all about. You want to be a member of the British Army and you are attracted to what it has to offer. If you have been pushed into joining by your family then you shouldn't be applying.

Sample response to interview question 1

Why do you want to join the Army?

I have wanted to join the Army for a number of years and feel that I have now reached a stage of my life where I am ready to commit to the service. Having studied the Army recruitment literature and visited the Army website, I am impressed by the professionalism and standards the service sets itself.

I would like a career that is fulfilling, challenging and rewarding and I believe that the Army would provide all of these. I enjoy keeping physically fit and active and believe that given the right training I would make a great team member. I am also very much attracted to the fact that the Army offers a wide choice of careers.

The fact that I would be improving my education and ending up with a trade is just another example of why I want to join the service. I have seriously considered the implications that joining a service such as the Army would have on both my personal life and social life and have discussed these with my family. They have given me their full support and commitment in helping me to achieve my goal of joining the Army.

Sample interview question 2

What does your family think of you wanting to join the Army?

Again, you are likely to be asked a question surrounding your family background and what they think about you wanting to join the Army. It is important that your family support you in your decision.

If they have any doubts about you joining the service then you may wish to consider taking them along to the AFCO so they can ask any questions or raise any concerns that they may have. When answering questions such as this it is important that you are honest and tell the truth. If your family have any concerns then share them with the Careers Officer, who will then be able to advise you on the best way for your family/partner to overcome any fears they may have.

Sample response to interview question 2

What does your family think of you wanting to join the Army?

I have discussed the issue with my family in depth and also shown them all of the Army recruitment literature to try to dampen any fears that they may have.

They were initially concerned about me joining but they gave me their full support after I told them everything I know about the training I will go through and the conditions I will serve under. They are aware that the Army has a good reputation and this has helped them to further understand why I want to join. They have seen how enthusiastic I am about wanting to join the Army and know that it will be great for me. I have also discussed the issue with my partner and he/she is extremely supportive. They are all looking forward to hopefully seeing me at my passing out parade if I am successful, and therefore I have their full backing.

Sample interview question 3

How do you think you will cope with Army life in relation to the discipline and being part of a military organisation?

When you join the Army you will be joining a military organisation that has set procedures, standards and discipline codes. To some people this will come as a shock and the Army wants to know that you are prepared for this change in lifestyle. It is investing time, effort and resources into your training so it wants to know that you can cope with the way of life.

When answering this type of question you need to demonstrate both your awareness of what Army life involves and also your positive attitude towards the disciplined environment. Study the recruitment literature and visit the Army website to get a feel for the type of training you will be going through.

Sample response to interview question 3

How do you think you will cope with Army life in relation to the discipline and being part of a military organisation?

Having read the information available to me about the Army way of life I think I would cope very well. I know that I will find it difficult at times but believe I have both the maturity and stability to succeed and become a competent member of the team. The very nature of the Army means that it requires a disciplined workforce. Without that discipline things can go wrong. If I am successful and do not carry out my duties professionally then I could endanger somebody's life. I understand why discipline is required and believe I would cope with it well. I understand that being in the Army isn't a nine-to-five job, but instead you must take on tasks whenever required.

In order to prepare for the training I have already integrated routine and self-discipline into my life. For example, I have been getting up at 6a.m. every weekday morning to go running

and I have started carrying out daily household tasks such as hoovering, cleaning and ironing. At the start of my preparation for joining the Army I made myself an action plan that would focus my mind on what I needed to do in order to improve.

Sample interview question 4

How do you think you will cope with being away from home and losing your personal freedom?

This type of question is one that needs to be answered positively. There is only one correct answer to this question and you need to demonstrate that you have considered the consequences of leaving home and are fully aware of what is involved. If you have any experience of being away from home then you should state this in your response. Try to think of occasions when you have been away for periods of time and tell the interviewers that it wasn't an issue.

Have you ever been a part of any youth organisations? If you have then this will undoubtedly go in your favour. Giving an example is far better than just saying you will be able to cope.

Sample response to interview question 4

How do you think you will cope with being away from home and losing your personal freedom?

Having already had experience of being away from home, I believe I would cope extremely well. Whilst serving with the Scouts a few years ago I was introduced to the Army way of life and fully understand what it is like to be away from home. I actually enjoy being away from home and I can't wait to get started if I am successful during selection. I understand however that the training is difficult and intense and I am fully prepared for this. I am confident that I will cope with the change in lifestyle very well and I am looking forward to the challenge if I am accepted.

Sample interview question 5

Are you involved in any sporting activities and how do you keep yourself fit?

When answering questions based around your own physical fitness you need to be honest but bear in mind the following points.

Although you don't have to be super fit to join the Army, you do need to have a good level of physical fitness, so being fit in the first instance is an obvious advantage. The Army, just like the other Armed Forces, prides itself on its ability to work as an effective team unit. Those people who engage in active team sports are more likely to be competent team members. If you play a team sport then this will be a good thing to tell the interviewers. If you don't then it may be a good idea to go and join one! Regardless of the above points, remember that if you don't do any physical activity whatsoever then you will score low in this area. Make sure you partake in some form of physical activity. During the ADSC you will be required to carry out a 1.5-mile run which should be your 'best effort'. The Army has realised that those people who cannot complete the run in less than 14 minutes are far more likely to suffer from injury during the initial training course. Start running now so that you can easily pass the forthcoming physical tests.

Sample response to interview question 5

Are you involved in any sporting activities and how do you keep yourself fit?

Yes, I am. I currently play in the local hockey team and have been doing that for a number of years now. Maintaining a good level of fitness is something I enjoy. In fact, recently I have increased my fitness levels by going swimming three times a week. I'm aware that during the recruit training course I will be pushed to my limits so I need to be prepared for

that. I believe the fact that I play team sports will help me get through my training.

I enjoy playing in a hockey team because when we are being beaten by another team everyone always pulls together and we work hard to try to win the game back. After the game we all meet in the club bar for a drink and chat about the game. Keeping fit is important to me and something that I want to continue doing throughout my career if I am successful in joining the Army.

Sample interview question 6

How do you think you will fit into a team environment?

Once again, it would be a positive thing if you can demonstrate you have experience of working in a team. Maybe you have experience of working in a sporting team or need to work as a team in your current job? Think of examples where you have already been working in a team environment and if you can provide an example where the team achieved something, then even better. Structure your answer around your own experiences and also around your knowledge of the fact that the Army needs to work as an effective team unit in order for it to complete its tasks both safely and on time.

Sample response to interview question 6

How do you think you will fit into a team environment?

I have experience of working in a team and I really enjoyed it, so I know I would fit in well. I play for my local rugby team and it is important that everybody gels together in order to win our games. The real test for the team is when we are being beaten and I always try to rally the team together and get us motivated to win back the points we have lost. I understand that the Army needs its people to work together effectively as a team to get the right result. If the team doesn't perform then people's lives can be put at risk. Being an effective part of the

team also means that I would have to train hard and keep up my competency levels, which I believe I would do well.

With my experience of team sports and having the ability to pull a team together when the chips are down, I think I would be a great asset to the Army team.

Sample interview question 7

What do you do in your spare time?

With questions of this nature the Army recruitment staff are looking to see if you use your leisure time wisely. Your response will tell them a lot about your attitude and motivation. We all know that some people spend their spare time doing nothing or watching TV and playing computer games. When you join the Army you won't have much time to sit around and do nothing. The Army will want to hear that you are active and doing worthwhile things during your spare time. For example, if you are involved in any sports, outdoor activities or are part of any youth organisation such as the Army Cadets then these are good things to tell the interviewers. You may also be involved in voluntary work or charity work and once again these will work in your favour if mentioned at interview.

If you currently do very little with your spare time then now is a good time to make a lifestyle change. Embark on a fitness routine or join an activity club or organisation.

Sample response to interview question 7

What do you do in your spare time?

During my spare time I like to keep active, both physically and mentally. I enjoy visiting the gym three times a week and I have a structured workout that I try to vary every three months to keep my interest levels up. I'm also currently doing a part-time study course in Art, which is one of my hobbies. I'm also a member of the local Army Cadets, which is an evening's commitment every week and the occasional weekend.

Of course, I know when it is time to relax and usually do this by either listening to music or playing snooker with my friends, but overall I'm quite an active person. I certainly don't like sitting around doing nothing. I understand that if I'm successful at joining the Army there will be plenty of things to do in the evenings to keep me occupied such as the gym and other various social events.

Sample interview question 8

Can you tell us about any personal achievements you have experienced during your life so far?

Having achieved something in your life demonstrates that you have the ability to see things through to the end. It also shows that you are motivated and determined to succeed. The Army wants to see evidence that you can achieve, as there is a greater chance of you completing the initial recruit course if you have a history of achievement. Try to think of examples where you have succeeded or achieved something relevant in your life. Some good examples of achievements are: Duke of Edinburgh's Award; A-levels or educational qualifications; team or individual sports awards/trophies/ medals; raising money for charity. Obviously you will have your own achievements that you will want to add in your response.

Sample response to interview question 8

Can you tell us about any personal achievements you have experienced during your life so far?

So far in my life I have managed to achieve a number of things that I am proud of. To begin with, I recently worked hard to achieve my GCSE results, which enabled me to go on to further education and study my choice of subject. Without these grades I would not have been able to do that.

About a year ago the football team that I play in won the league trophy for the second year running, which is another one of my more recent achievements.

However, my most memorable achievement to date is managing to raise £1,000 for a local charity. I worked hard and ran a marathon in order to raise the money. I was particularly proud of this achievement because It meant the charity I ran for was able to purchase some important items of equipment that could be used to treat some of its patients.

Sample interview question 9

What are your strengths?

This is a common interview question, which is relatively easy to answer. The problem with it is that many people use the same response. It is quite an easy thing to tell the interviewer that you are dedicated and the right person for the job. However, it is a different thing backing it up with evidence!

If you are asked this type of question make sure you are positive during your response and show that you actually mean what you are saying. Then, back your answer up with examples of when you have demonstrated a strength that you say you have. For example, if you tell the panel that you are a motivated person, then back it up with an event in your life where you achieved something through sheer motivation and determination.

Sample response to interview question 9

What are your strengths?

To begin with I am a determined person who likes to see things through to the end. For example, I recently ran a marathon for charity. I'd never done this kind of thing before and found it very hard work, but I made sure I completed the task. Another strength of mine is that I'm always looking for ways to improve myself.

As an example, I have been preparing for the Army selection process by performing lots of mock maths tests. I noticed that I was getting a number of questions wrong. In order to improve I decided to get some personal tuition at my college to ensure that I could pass this part of the selection process.

Finally, I would say that one of my biggest strengths is that I'm a great team player. I really enjoy working in a team environment and achieving things through a collaborative approach. For example, I play in a local rugby team and we recently won the league trophy for the first time since the club was established some 50 years ago.

Sample interview question 10

What is your biggest weakness?

Now there's a question! If we were all totally honest with ourselves we could probably write a whole list of weaknesses. Now I wouldn't advise that you reel off a whole list of weaknesses in your interview as you could do yourself a lot of harm. Conversely, those people who say that they don't have any weaknesses are probably not telling the truth.

If you are asked a question of this nature then it is important that you give at least one weakness. The trick here is to make the weakness sound like a strength. For example, a person may say that one of their weaknesses is that their own personal standards are too high sometimes and they expect this level from others. Or another one is that a person doesn't know when to relax. They are always on the go achieving and making things happen when they should take more time out to relax and recuperate.

Sample response to interview question 10

What is your biggest weakness?

That's a difficult question but I know that I do have a particular weakness. The standards that I always set myself are quite

high and unfortunately I get frustrated when other people's aren't. For example, I am hardly ever late for anything and believe that punctuality is important. However, if I'm left waiting for other people who are late I usually have to say something to them when they finally arrive, which isn't always a good thing. I need to understand that not everyone is the same and let some things go over my head.

Sample interview question II

Can you tell me what you have learnt about your chosen career?

Once again, an almost guaranteed question so make sure you have prepared for it fully. When preparing for this type of question I would recommend that you visit the Army website and also study carefully your recruitment literature. You need to find out the type and length of training you would be expected to undertake for your chosen career. This information will be available through your Armed Forces Careers adviser. The sample response that I have provided here is for somebody who is hoping to join as an Aircraft Dispatcher. Use the example to create your own response relevant to your own chosen career. You may even wish to look at other avenues of research to improve your knowledge and further demonstrate your determination to succeed. For example, if you are wishing to join as a chef then why not buy a book relating to cookery or embark on an evening class and start learning before you even join!

Sample response to interview question 11

Can you tell me what you have learnt about your chosen career?

Chosen career – Aircraft Dispatcher

I understand that the Army relies on air delivery from helicopters and other transport aircraft to re-supply quickly. My job as an Aircraft Dispatcher would be to make sure the loads are

carried safely and delivered in one piece. It doesn't matter whether the loads are slung underneath a Chinook helicopter or dropped by parachute from a Hercules aircraft, it would still be my responsibility to ensure things went smoothly.

I would be working with other services such as the Royal Air Force and I would be travelling with my cargo most of the time. In addition to my main role as Aircraft Dispatcher I would also learn to drive and be trained in survival, safety and emergency drills.

Sample interview question 12

What qualities do you think you need to be a good team player?

The Army needs effective and competent team players. If you already have some experience of working in a team environment then this will work in your favour. Try to think of examples where you have already successfully contributed to a team task either at work or during your education. There are many different qualities required to work as an effective team player. Here are just a few: being enthusiastic; a good communicator; motivated; supportive of the other team members; providing other team members with encouragement; determined to complete the task; professional and competent; always focused on the wider team objective.

Now take a look at the following sample response to this question.

Sample response to interview question 12

What qualities do you think you need to be a good team player?

First of all I believe a team player must be focused purely on the task that the team is trying to achieve. You must always be professional and supportive of the other team members.

For example, if one of the team members is struggling then you should try to help them and support them with their role within the team. It is important as a team player to listen to the brief or details of the task and to communicate properly with everyone else in the team. You must always put the needs of the team before your own and be totally committed to completing the task in hand.

Sample interview question 13

What contact have you had with the Army during your application and what have you done to find out about Army life?

Those applicants who are serious about a career in the Army will have gone out of their way to find out about the service and what it involves. The Army recruitment staff will want to see evidence that you have taken steps to speak to people who are already serving and that you have researched the organisation effectively. It is important that you are 100 per cent committed to joining and that you are fully aware of the challenge that lies ahead of you.

Sample response to interview question 13

What contact have you had with the Army during your application and what have you done to find out about Army life?

During my preparation I have carried out lots of research into the Army so that I am fully aware of the challenge that lies ahead of me. To begin with I have studied my recruitment literature in depth and I have also spent plenty of time browsing the Army recruitment website. I have also obtained a copy of the British Army Pocket Guide which has taught me lots about the service, the regiments and the equipment. More recently I spent a couple of hours at my local Army establishment where I managed to speak to serving soldiers and officers about their role and the job. I found this an

invaluable insight. All of this research and reading has made me more excited about joining. I cannot wait to get started if I am successful.

Sample interview question 14

What are the values of the British Army?

During one of the early chapters of this book I made reference to the Army values. Every soldier and officer is expected to abide by these important values and therefore it is not unreasonable for the Army to expect you to know them when you apply. You are likely to be asked a question that relates to the values during the ADSC interview so make sure you know them and what each one of them means.

Sample response to interview question 14

What are the values of the British Army?

The values of the British Army are a selfless commitment, courage, discipline, integrity, loyalty and respect for others. As a soldier you have to be prepared to carry out tasks that others don't have to. It is important to be strong and aggressive in battle but to also behave properly and demonstrate self-control at all times. Being courageous means facing up to danger and doing what is right at all times. Discipline means having the ability to maintain constant high standards, so that others can rely on you. Integrity means earning the respect and trust of your work colleagues. Loyalty is being faithful to your work colleagues and to your duty and having respect for others means treating everybody with respect and dignity at all times.

Sample interview question 15

What are you currently doing in order to prepare for your training?

Whilst this question should be generally easy to answer, it does end up throwing many applicants. Most people who apply to join the Army will do little or no preparation for basic training until they have received confirmation that they have passed the ADSC. However, if you can show the Army Development Selection Officer at ADSC and even the Careers Officer that you are already preparing for basic training then this will impress them. Here is a sample response to assist you.

Sample response to interview question 15

What are you currently doing in order to prepare for your training?

Although I haven't yet passed selection I have been preparing thoroughly for my basic training as I want to ensure I am fully prepared. To begin with I have created a timetable of preparation which makes sure I work on my weak areas and my overall fitness. Every weekday I am up at 6a.m. and I embark on a 4-mile run. This is so that I can get used to the early starts and so that I can improve my fitness levels. Half way round my run I always make sure I stop and carry out 50 press-ups and 50 sit-ups. When I get home from work I then sit down for an hour and work on my knowledge of the Army and the branch that I am applying for. Every other day I work on my aptitude test ability and I make sure I read a good quality newspaper so that I am up to date with Army operations and the more important current affairs issues. Finally, I have been working on my household skills such as ironing and cleaning.

Sample interview question 16

Can you tell me what your basic training and branch training will involve, where it will take place and how long it will last?

Before you attend your interview you must find out details about your initial training and also your chosen regiment/ branch training including: where the training will take place; what the training involves (weekly breakdown); how long it will last.

The above information will be available through your AFCO Adviser and there will also be information within your recruitment literature and on the Army website (www. armyjobs.mod.uk).

Please note: the following sample response is based on an individual who is entering the Army at over the age of 17 years. It is important to confirm with your AFCO Adviser the type, location and duration of training that you will be required to undertake for your particular regiment/branch.

Sample response to interview question 16

Can you tell me what your basic training and branch training will involve, where it will take place and how long it will last?

My initial basic training will take place at Catterick and it will last for 12 weeks. During this time I will learn all about Army life and in particular weapon handling skills, map reading, administration, physical fitness, health and safety, field-craft and navigation to name just a few subjects. After successful completion of the six-week phase I will complete the 'Passing of the Square' when I will be awarded with the honour of wearing the 'Caubeen' our regimental headdress.

Once I have completed my initial 12-week course and successfully passed out it will be on to phase 2 training. This will also take place at Catterick. The first 14 weeks of phase 2

training I will learn how to operate all different types of Infantry weapon systems and also learn how to integrate field-craft skills with each particular weapon.

During my research and my talks with serving soldiers I understand that tactical training will play a big part of my Infantry training. I will take part in a large number of field exercises where I will learn about tactics and modern warfare. At the end of my training I will be competent at patrolling during both day and night and be able to use optical viewing aids, radios and satellite navigation devices. Towards the end of my phase 2 training I will need to pass a difficult two-week infantry field firing camp. This is where I will need to demonstrate everything I have learnt during my entire training.

Once I have successfully passed everything I will have gained an Education Certificate in Public Service, NVQ Level 1. Following pass out I will then go on to join my regiment.

Sample interview question 17

Tell me about your educational exam results. Were you satisfied with them and what did you think of your teachers and your school?

Many people leave school without the grades that they want. I was one of them! However, it's my opinion that what you do following your exam results is the most important thing. Despite only achieving three GCSEs at grade C or above I went on to achieve many qualifications after my initial school education was over. Apart from many Fire Service qualifications I more recently achieve a Diploma in Management and various health and safety qualifications. The point I am trying to make here is that you can still achieve many things in life despite poor educational qualifications.

This question is designed to see what you personally think about your results and also your attitude to your education and people (teachers), who are in positions of authority. If you didn't get the results that you wanted then just say so.

However, it is important to tell the interviewer what you plan to do about them and what your plans are for the future. When I passed Armed Forces selection many years ago I had a six-month wait before I could start my basic training. The Warrant Officer at the AFCO advised that I embarked on an educational foundation course at college for the six-month period whilst I waited to start my basic training. I took his advice and I am glad that I did. Whilst responding to this interview question be positive about the future and tell the interviewers what you are currently doing to improve your academic skills. Tell them how hard you have been working for the BARB tests and what steps you have taken to study and prepare for Army selection.

The second part of the question is very important. As I discussed at the beginning of this book the Army will be assessing your reaction to discipline and regimentation. Those candidates who are disrespectful to their parents, teachers or people in positions of authority are very unlikely to pass selection. Be careful what you say and always demonstrate a mature and professional image to the interviewer.

Sample response to interview question 17

Tell me about your educational exam results. Were you satisfied with them and what did you think of your teachers and your school?

I did OK in the majority of exams but I wasn't satisfied with my Maths result. I know I could have done better. However, since my results I've working hard to improve my skills in this area and I've embarked on an evening course which will hopefully gain me a better grade. I'm a determined person and I'm always looking to improve my skills. One of my strengths is that I can see what I need to work on and always make sure I work hard to make the necessary improvements.

In relation to my teachers and my school I have a lot of respect for them. The teachers are in positions of authority and it is important to respect that.

Interview question 18

What contract will you be under if you are successful and what are your discharge options?

This question is sometimes asked so that the Army can be certain you are fully aware of the commitment you will need to make. If you don't know the minimum contract terms and the discharge options then make sure you find out before you attend your interview.

Sample response to interview question 18

What contract will you be under if you are successful and what are your discharge option?

Because I am over 18 years old my contract time is four years and three months. If I want to leave after this point then I will have to give 12 months' notice in writing. If I wish to stay on after the initial four years and three months then I can leave at any time providing that I give the 12 months' notice in writing. I am aware that the maximum I can serve is 22 years.

With regards to discharge options I have to serve 28 days of initial training. After the 28th day I can write to the Army and request to leave. After this time I am committed to serving my contract.

Top interview tips for both AFCO and ADSC interviews

- When you walk into the interview room stand up straight with your shoulders back. Project an image of confidence.

- Don't sit down in the interview chair until invited to do so.

- Sit with your hands resting on your knees, palms downwards. It is OK to use your hands expressively but don't overdo it.

(Continued)

 how2become

(Continued)

- Don't slouch in the chair.

- Speak up and be positive.

- Smile, be happy and have a sense of humour.

- Dress as smartly as you can and take a pride in your appearance. If you don't have a suit make sure you wear a shirt and tie at the very least.

- Improve your personal hygiene and cleanliness. Make sure you have showered and that your hands and nails are clean.

- Make sure you have researched both the Army life and your chosen career/careers. This is very important.

- During the interview do not be negative or disrespectful towards your teachers, parents or people in positions of authority. Remember that you are applying to join a disciplined service.

- Go the extra mile and learn a little bit about the Army's history if you get time. When the panel ask you 'What can you tell us about the Army?', you will be able to demonstrate that you have made an effort to look into its history as well as its modern day activities.

- Be respectful and courteous towards the interview panel. At the end of your response to each question finish off with either 'Sir' or 'Ma'am', or as otherwise instructed.

- Ask positive questions at the end of the interview. Try not to ask questions such as 'How much leave will I get?' or 'How often do I get paid?'

- If you are unsure about a question don't waffle. If you do not know the answer then it is OK to say so. Move on to the next question and put it behind you.

- Finally, believe in yourself and be confident. A positive attitude will bring positive results!

THE BRITISH ARMY
RECRUIT BATTERY TEST

CHAPTER 6

INTRODUCTION TO THE BARB TEST AND PRACTICE QUESTIONS

So far within this book we have covered a large number of topics that relate to your preparation and mental approach towards the selection process. Over the next few chapters we will set to work on improving your ability to pass the different stages.

One of the initial stages of the selection process will require you to sit the British Army Recruit Battery test, more commonly known as the 'BARB test', which has been in use for many years. It is a tried and tested method that the Army will use to determine what career(s) you are most likely to be suited for. It is important that you aim for the highest score possible on the test and this can only be achieved through 'deliberate' and 'repetitive' practice.

The pass mark for the BARB test is currently 26 although you will need to confirm this with your local Armed Forces Careers Office (AFCO). This effectively means that you must

get 26 questions correct, but as I mentioned earlier don't just settle for a pass. You need to achieve as high a score as possible as this will give you more career options depending on your academic results.

Work hard at practising the tests within this book and also within the BARB booklet when you receive it from the AFCO. Don't just sit back like so many people do – practise hard and make sure you pass. Your choice of trade will be dependent upon the score you achieve during the BARB test. Basically, the higher your score, the more career options you will have. This is a good incentive therefore for you to work hard and prepare fully.

It is also important that you follow my previous advice on creating the right impression. It may not seem appropriate to dress smartly when you are attending the BARB test but that little bit of extra effort in terms of your appearance and bearing will go a long way to aid your mental preparation.

More about the BARB test

Psychometric tests within the British Army are used as a tool to measure the mind and your ability. If we break down the word 'psychometric' we can see that 'psycho' means mind and 'metric' means to measure. BARB is a computer-based, psychometric assessment that was developed by the Defence Evaluation and Research Agency (DERA) and Plymouth University. It is a series of timed questions that assess a candidate's ability to absorb information quickly and logically. The computer automatically calculates the candidate's score, based on the number of correct answers and the time taken. The final score is referred to as the GTI (General Trainability Index). The BARB test has been in use since July 1992.

In order to prepare effectively for BARB test study, the following pages provide you with a host of sample test questions. Another great way to help you practise is to purchase your own psychometric testing booklet. These are available from www.how2become.co.uk.

Tips for improving your BARB test scores

- Once you have completed your BARB test preparation there are still a number of things you can do in order to improve your scores. It is vital that you get a good night's sleep the night before you are due to take the test. There are many reasons for this but the main one is that you will give yourself a better chance of achieving a higher score. This in turn will give you more career options to choose from. It will also ensure that you feel confident before taking the test as fatigue can cause stress, which will inhibit your performance on the day.

- Make sure that you know exactly where you need to go to take the test. This may sound like an obvious tip but you'll be amazed at how many people get to the test centre late and are then not allowed to sit the test. Go to the test centre a few days before your scheduled date to familiarise yourself fully with the directions and parking facilities, etc.

- Do not take the test on an empty stomach. You should try to eat a good breakfast on the morning of your test. This doesn't mean eating a great big fry-up but instead eating something that is light and that will give you sustained energy throughout the day. A bowl of porridge is great for providing sustained energy or try a healthy cereal such as bran flakes with a chopped banana spread over the top.

- If your test is scheduled to start at 10a.m. make sure you get there early enough to avoid a last minute panic. It is far better to get there early and have to hang around rather than get there late and not be able to sit the test at all.

- Take a small bottle of water with you to keep yourself hydrated and focused.

(Continued)

(Continued)

- If you wear glasses make sure you take them along with you. You will be using a computer and you need to ensure you can see correctly.

- The night before the test read any correspondence thoroughly at least twice and make sure you haven't missed anything glaringly obvious. You may be required to take something with you and if you don't do what is required it shows that you are not very good at following instructions – something that is key to a soldier's role.

- What dress code would you expect and what dress code would you be most impressed with? Remember that you are joining a disciplined service that always looks smart and prepared. Just because you are not a soldier yet, doesn't mean to say you can't start thinking like one. Go smartly dressed, which will present a good image.

CHAPTER 7
REASONING TEST

Within this chapter I have provided you with a number of sample test questions to help you prepare for the real test. Please note that these are not the exact questions that you will be required to sit on the day. However, they are a useful practice tool in order to help focus your mind on the type of tests you will be sitting. It is also important to point out that during the real test you will be required to answer the questions on a computer screen and how they will be presented will be different from how they are formatted within this book.

Take a look at the explanations provided and make sure you fully understand what is involved before attempting the practice questions. Once you have completed the practice questions it is important that you take note of where you have gone wrong. Learn from any mistakes as this will help you to improve your scores during the real test.

Reasoning tests form an integral part of the BARB selection tests within the British Army selection process. These tests are relatively simple to understand once you fully appreciate what is required. The reasoning tests are basically a form of

problem solving and you will be asked a number of questions, usually about a relationship between two people. For example, you could be asked a question along the following lines.

Sample question I

Richard is taller than Steven. Who is shorter?

The answer in this case would be Steven as the statement suggests that Richard is taller than Steven. Therefore Steven is the shorter of the two.

Answer: *Steven*

Here is another example.

Sample question 2

Mark is not as wealthy as Jane. Who has less money?

The statement suggests that Mark is not as wealthy as Jane therefore suggesting that Jane has more money. Mark therefore has less money and is not as wealthy as Jane.

Answer: *Mark*.

When you are answering these questions it is important that you READ each question thoroughly. The questions are relatively simple to answer but they can catch you out if you do not understand *exactly* what the question is asking.

Tips for passing the reasoning tests

When you attend the careers office to sit the BARB test you may be asked to take the test on a computer. The computer version of the test will require you to use 'touch screen' answers, which means that instead of using a pen and paper to mark down your answers you will have to touch the computer screen instead. Whilst this is far quicker than writing down your answers, you will need to understand the questions fully before giving your answer.

The question on the screen may appear as a statement, as follows:

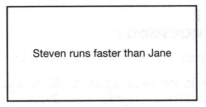

Once you have read the statement you will then need to touch the screen to obtain the question. Make certain that you remember the statement as when you touch the screen it will disappear and you will be given two choices of answer as follows:

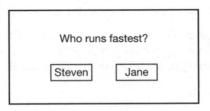

Once the question appears you will then be required to touch the screen in order to indicate your answer. Can you remember what the statement was? My tip is to repeat the statement at least three times in your head before touching the screen to obtain the question. Once the question appears you can repeat the statement to yourself that **Steven runs faster than Jane** and therefore provide yourself with the answer to the question – *Steven is the fastest.*

Once you fully understand what is required, move on to Exercise 1 on the following page. You have 5 minutes in which to answer the 15 questions. Please note that the time limit placed on this exercise will not be the same as the one set during the real BARB test.

Once you have completed the exercise make sure you check thoroughly any questions you got wrong. It is important to do this so that you can improve on your scores during the real test

Reasoning test: Exercise 1

Question 1

Marcus is not as bright as Andrew. Who is brighter?

Answer

Question 2

Sharon is taller than Sheila. Who is the tallest?

Answer

Question 3

Pauline is stronger than Beverley. Who is the weaker of the two?

Answer

Question 4

Gary is lighter than Fred. Who is the heavier?

Answer

Question 5

The black car is faster than the white car. Which car is the quickest?

Answer

Question 6

Rachel runs faster than her sister Georgia. Who runs the slowest?

Answer

Question 7

David has more money than Arnold. Who is the poorer?

Answer

Question 8

Jill is weaker than Bill. Who is the strongest?

Answer

Question 9

Hayley sleeps for 10 hours and Julie sleeps for 650 minutes. Who sleeps the longest?

Answer

Question 10

Sadie's shoe size is 7 and Mary's is 9. Who needs the larger size shoes?

Answer

Question 11

George is sadder than Mark. Who is the happier of the two?

Answer

Question 12

Pete is faster than Rick. Who is the slowest?

Answer

Question 13

Jim is older than Brian. Who is the youngest?

Answer

Question 14

Katie eats more slowly than Lucy. Who is the faster eater?

Answer

Question 15

John finishes the race before Tony. Who ran the slowest?

Answer

Now that you have completed Exercise 1, take the time to check over your answers carefully. If you got any of them wrong then make sure you learn from your mistakes. This is a crucial part of your development. Once you are satisfied move on to the next exercise.

Answers to Reasoning test: Exercise 1

1. Andrew
2. Sharon
3. Beverley
4. Fred
5. The black car
6. Georgia
7. Arnold
8. Bill
9. Julie
10. Mary
11. Mark
12. Rick
13. Brian
14. Lucy
15. Tony

Reasoning test: Exercise 2

Question I

The red car is twice as fast as the grey car. Which car is slowest?

Answer

Question 2

Julia is half the weight of her neighbour Jonathan. Who is the heaviest?

Answer

Question 3

Barry has been playing darts for three times longer than his team mate Paul. Who has played for the least amount of time?

Answer

Question 4

Jim passed his driving test in 1998 and his wife Gloria passed hers in 1989. Who has held their driving licence the longest?

Answer

Question 5

Darren lives 13 miles away from his place of work. Jessica's workplace is 12 miles away from her home? Who lives the furthest away from their place of work?

Answer

Question 6

Rupert has a motorbike which cost £6,450 and Mark has a motorbike which cost £5,654. Who has the least expensive motorbike?

Answer

Question 7

Ronald weighs slightly more than Peter. Who is the lightest?

Answer

Question 8

Stuart's house was built in August 1965 and his girlfriend Margaret's house was built in January 1965. Whose house is the oldest?

Answer

Question 9

If Jen has £3.95 and Marcus has 295 pence, who has the least money?

Answer

Question 10

Carol attends the doctor's surgery at 9a.m. and leaves at 9.35a.m. Harriet attends the doctor's surgery at 9.35a.m. and leaves at 10.09a.m. Who stayed at the doctor's for the least amount of time?

Answer

Question 11

Ben joined the Army on October the 3rd 1997 and left nine years later. Hannah joined the Army on January the 25th 1993 and left on January the 25th 2003. Who stayed in the Army the longest?

Answer

Question 12

In 2005 a total of 11,400 people joined the Army. In the previous year a total 10,340 joined the Army. In which of the two years did the Army recruit the least amount of people?

Answer

Question 13

Abdi is wealthier than Maggie. Who is the poorest?

Answer

Question 14

Stuart rides his bike at twice the speed of Simon. Who rides their bike the fastest?

Answer

Question 15

Michelle takes out a mortgage for £189,500 and Anthony takes out a mortgage for £198,200. Who has the least amount to pay back?

Answer

Once again, take the time to check over your answers carefully correcting any that you have got wrong before moving onto the next exercise.

Answers to Reasoning test: Exercise 2

1. The grey car
2. Jonathan
3. Paul
4. Gloria
5. Darren
6. Mark
7. Peter
8. Margaret's house
9. Marcus
10. Carol
11. Hannah
12. 2004
13. Maggie
14. Stuart
15. Michelle

Reasoning test: Exercise 3

Question 1

Bill got 70 per cent of his answers correct during the test while Sam got 25 per cent incorrect. Who achieved the highest score in the test?

Answer

Question 2

Richard is not as happy as Graham. Who is the happier?

Answer

Question 3

William has a car that is half as fast as Bill's. Who has the slowest car?

Answer

Question 4

Anthony can run twice as fast as Hillary. Who is the slowest runner?

Answer

Question 5

Jean was born in 1971 and Frank was born three years later. Who is the eldest?

Answer

Question 6

Peter washed his car for 90 minutes whereas Abdul washed his for one hour and 20 minutes. Who washed his car for the longest?

Answer

Question 7

Ahmed is more intelligent than Sinita. Who is the brightest?

Answer

Question 8

Mika passed his motorbike test 18 months ago whereas June passed her motorbike test 350 days ago. Who passed their test first?

Answer

Question 9

Fin carries five bags of shopping home and Dalton carries home seven. Who has the least number of bags to carry?

Answer

Question 10

Naomi arrives at work at 0834 hours and leaves at 1612 hours. Stuart arrives at work at 0915 hours and leaves at 1700 hours. Who stayed at work for the least amount of time?

Answer

Question 11

Preston weighs heavier than Paris. Who is the lightest?

Answer [   ]

Question 12

David is not as good as Brian. Who is better?

Answer [   ]

Question 13

Ricky is not as fast as Carlos. Who is the fastest?

Answer [   ]

Question 14

Yasmin is sadder than Beatrice. Who is happier?

Answer [   ]

Question 15

Laurence is poorer than Gene. Who is richer?

Answer [   ]

Once again, take the time to check over your answers, carefully correcting any that you have got wrong before moving onto the next section of the BARB test.

Answers to Reasoning test: Exercise 3

1. Sam
2. Graham
3. William
4. Hillary
5. Jean
6. Abdul
7. Ahmed
8. Mika
9. Fin
10. Naomi
11. Paris
12. Brian
13. Carlos
14. Beatrice
15. Gene

CHAPTER 8
THE LETTER CHECKING TEST

When you come to sit the BARB test you will be asked to answer questions where you are required to check letters. The aim of this test is to see how fast you can check information that is presented to you. Whilst working in the Army you will often be required to carry out specific tasks which involve the accurate checking of information, equipment and data.

The following is an example of a letter checking question.

Sample question 1

How many letters match?

P	I	O	T	S
p	N	K	t	u

How many letters match?

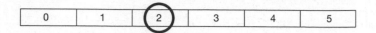

You can see from the above example that there are columns of letters. In the 1st and 4th boxes are letters that are identical, albeit one letter is a capital and the other is not. The other boxes contain different letters and therefore do not match. It is your task to identify how many pairs of letters match. In this case I have circled the correct answer for you as being 2 matching pairs.

During the real BARB test you will most probably be asked to sit the computer 'touch-screen' version of the test as opposed to writing down your answers.

When you carry out the test on the computer the question on the screen will be presented to you in a similar format to the following:

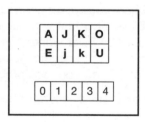

Below the provided letters will be a number of boxes giving you a choice of how many letters match. In this case the answer is 2 as the middle two columns of letters match, whereas the outer two do not. In this case you would touch the number '2' box as your answer. It is important that you work as quickly as possible as the more you score correctly, the higher your result will be at the end. As always, deliberate and repetitive practice will serve well to increase your scores.

Tips for improving your score on the Letter Checking test

When answering these questions you may find it useful to scan each line downwards in turn and keep a check of how many are correct. When you have scanned the final fourth line you will know how many are correct and then you can touch the number on the screen that corresponds to the right answer.

You will have very little time to answer as many as you can during the real test so you need to work quickly but as accurately as possible. Look out for letters that are similar but not the same, such as:

Q and O

G and Q

P and q

These are the ones that may catch you out so make sure you check carefully.

Now take a look at the first Letter Checking exercise on the following page and see how you get on. There are 15 questions and you have 5 minutes in which to answer them. Simply circle the correct answer with a pen or pencil.

Letter Checking test: Exercise 1

Question I

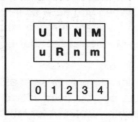

Question 2

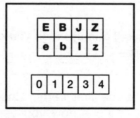

Question 3

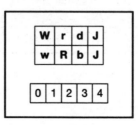

Question 4

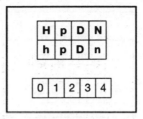

Question 5

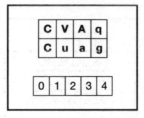

Question 6

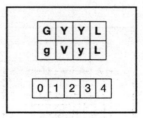

Question 7

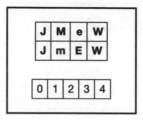

Question 8

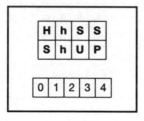

Question 9

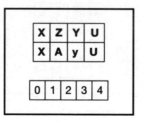

Question IO

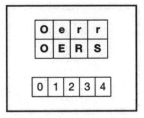

Question II

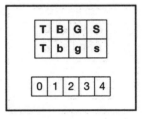

Question I2

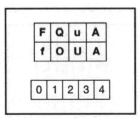

Question 13

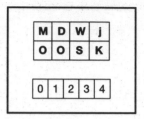

Question 14

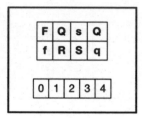

Question 15

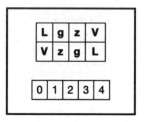

Now that you have completed the first Letter Checking exercise take the time to assess your performance against the answers below. If you got any wrong make sure you return to the question and see where you need to improve.

Once you are satisfied move on to Exercise 2.

Answers to Letter Checking test: Exercise 1

1.	3	**6.**	3	**11.**	4
2.	3	**7.**	4	**12.**	3
3.	3	**8.**	1	**13.**	0
4.	4	**9.**	3	**14.**	3
5.	2	**10.**	3	**15.**	0

Letter Checking test: Exercise 2

Question 1

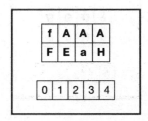

Question 2

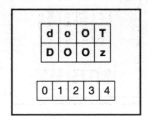

Question 3

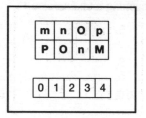

Question 4

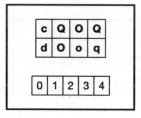

Question 5

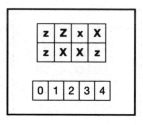

Question 6

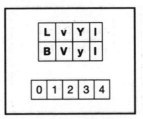

Question 7

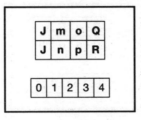

Question 8

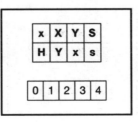

Question 9

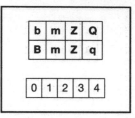

Question 10

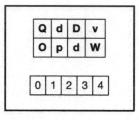

Question 11

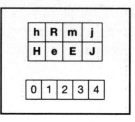

Question 12

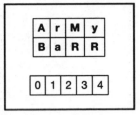

Question 13

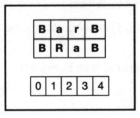

Question 14

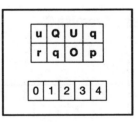

Question 15

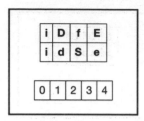

Once again, take the time to assess your performance against the answers below. If you got any wrong make sure you return to the question and see where you need to improve.

Once you are satisfied move on to the next exercise.

Answers to Letter Checking test: Exercise 2

1. 2		**6.** 3		**11.** 2
2. 3		**7.** 1		**12.** 0
3. 0		**8.** 1		**13.** 2
4. 2		**9.** 4		**14.** 1
5. 2		**10.** 1		**15.** 3

Letter Checking test: Exercise 3

Question 1

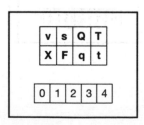

Question 2

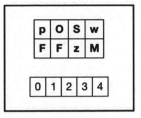

Question 3

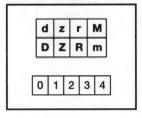

Question 4

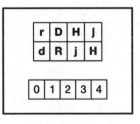

Question 5

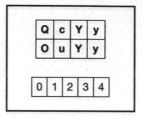

Question 6

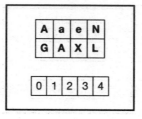

Question 7

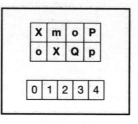

Question 8

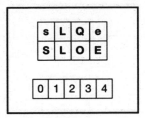

Question 9

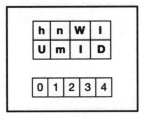

Question 10

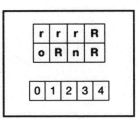

Question 11

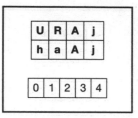

Question 12

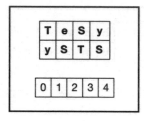

Question 13

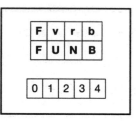

Question 14

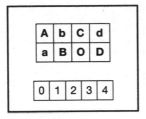

Question 15

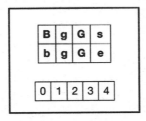

Once again, take the time to assess your performance against the answers below. If you got any wrong make sure you return to the question and see where you need to improve.

Once you are satisfied move on to the next section of the BARB test.

Answers to Letter Checking test: Exercise 3

1.	2	**6.**	1	**11.**	2
2.	0	**7.**	1	**12.**	0
3.	4	**8.**	3	**13.**	2
4.	0	**9.**	0	**14.**	3
5.	2	**10.**	2	**15.**	3

CHAPTER 9
THE DISTANCE NUMBER TEST

During the BARB test you will have to sit what is called a Distance Number test. This test requires you to analyse three numbers and decide which one of the three fits certain criteria. For example, you may find three numbers appear on your computer screen as follows:

$$7 \quad 10 \quad 14$$

The numbers can appear in any order and will not necessarily increase in value as indicated above. You then have to analyse the numbers and decide which one is the largest number and which one is the smallest. In this case:

- **largest value = 14**
- **smallest value = 7**

This then leaves you with the number 10. Once you have decided which number remains (in this case the number 10)

you then must decide which of the two numbers (7 or 14) is the *furthest* away from it, hence the title 'Distance Number' test. To work this out you can see that 7 is 3 away from 10 but 14 is 4 away from 10, therefore leaving you with the answer 14.

This may seem complicated at first but with a little practice you will soon grasp the concept of what is required. As with all types of assessment test, the best way to improve your score is to prepare and practise. Try as many practice questions as possible and you will find that your scores will keep increasing.

On the following pages are a number of sample questions to aid your preparation. Before you start the test take a look at the following four-step approach that will help you to answer the questions.

STEP 1
Out of the three numbers, decide which one is the smallest and which one is the largest.

↓

STEP 2
Then look at the number you are left with.

↓

STEP 3
Now decide which of the two numbers in step 1 is furthest away from the number in step 2

↓

STEP 4
The number that is the furthest away is your answer.

Now move on to Exercise 1. There are 30 questions for you to try and you have 15 minutes in which to answer them. Note that the times that are provided in this test are different from times allocated in the real test.

Distance Number test: Exercise 1

Question 1

3   7   9

Answer

Question 2

4   8   2

Answer

Question 3

1   3   4

Answer

Question 4

10   15   19

Answer

Question 5

6   2   9

Answer

Question 6

7   13   12

Answer

Question 7

67   87   106

Answer

Question 8

2   1   4

Answer

Question 9

> 12   6   1

Answer

Question 10

> 4   9   6

Answer

Question 11

> 5   10   16

Answer

Question 12

> 100   101   98

Answer

Question 13

2   4   8

Answer

Question 14

14   21   8

Answer

Question 15

99   108   120

Answer

Question 16

7   2   13

Answer

Question 17

14   17   12

Answer

Question 18

9   7   13

Answer

Question 19

11   22   31

Answer

Question 20

98   90   80

Answer

Question 21

```
5   3   8
```

Answer

Question 22

```
15   4   10
```

Answer

Question 23

```
65   60   72
```

Answer

Question 24

```
45   38   30
```

Answer

Question 25

12   8   3

Answer

Question 26

108   208   18

Answer

Question 27

7   13   5

Answer

Question 28

3   8   5

Answer

Question 29

19 6 13

Answer

Question 30

2 9 17

Answer

Now that you have completed the first Distance Number exercise work through your answers checking carefully to see which, if any, you got wrong.

Answers to Distance Number test: Exercise 1

1. 3	**11.** 16	**21.** 8
2. 8	**12.** 98	**22.** 4
3. 1	**13.** 8	**23.** 72
4. 10	**14.** 21	**24.** 30
5. 2	**15.** 120	**25.** 3
6. 7	**16.** 13	**26.** 208
7. 67	**17.** 17	**27.** 13
8. 4	**18.** 13	**28.** 8
9. 12	**19.** 11	**29.** 6
10. 9	**20.** 80	**30.** 17

Now move on to Exercise 2. Again, there are 30 questions for you to try and you have 15 minutes in which to answer

them. The times that are provided in this test are different from times allocated in the real test.

Distance Number test: Exercise 2

Question I

15   4   8

Answer

Question 2

2   6   9

Answer

Question 3

11   8   14

Answer

Question 4

1   19   3

Answer

Question 5

16 11 17

Answer

Question 6

8 3 9

Answer

Question 7

99 89 77

Answer

Question 8

267 16 134

Answer

Question 9

97   50   2

Answer

Question 10

45   44   42

Answer

Question 11

15   3   29

Answer

Question 12

66   14   33

Answer

Question 13

104	135	167

Answer

Question 14

474	300	122

Answer

Question 15

9	8	34

Answer

Question 16

90	45	3

Answer

Question 17

808   10   807

Answer

Question 18

1   55   101

Answer

Question 19

2   22   44

Answer

Question 20

65   99   128

Answer

Question 21

```
0   53   105
```

Answer

Question 22

```
36   2   17
```

Answer

Question 23

```
1001   501   2
```

Answer

Question 24

```
7   63   6
```

Answer

Question 25

809   799   698

Answer

Question 26

48   25   1

Answer

Question 27

5   16   25

Answer

Question 28

788   3   1574

Answer

Question 29

```
1000    100    599
```

Answer [   ]

Question 30

```
1971    11    1961
```

Answer [   ]

Now that you have completed Exercise 2 of the Distance Number test work through your answers once again checking carefully to see which, if any, you got wrong.

Answers to Distance Number test: Exercise 2

1.	15	**11.**	29	**21.**	0
2.	2	**12.**	66	**22.**	36
3.	14	**13.**	167	**23.**	1001
4.	19	**14.**	122	**24.**	63
5.	11	**15.**	34	**25.**	698
6.	3	**16.**	90	**26.**	1
7.	77	**17.**	10	**27.**	5
8.	267	**18.**	1	**28.**	1574
9.	2	**19.**	44	**29.**	100
10.	42	**20.**	65	**30.**	11

CHAPTER 10
THE PRACTICE NUMERACY TEST

The Distance Number test, as previously stated, is designed to test your ability to quickly and accurately perform tasks in your head. A good way to practise is to carry out basic addition and subtraction exercises without the aid of a calculator. You will find that just by carrying out a 10-minute exercise each day you will improve your response times greatly.

On the following pages are some numerical reasoning tests to assist you in your preparation. Please note that these tests are *not* the type that you will come across in the BARB test and they should be used as a practice facility only. There are 30 questions for you to work through and you have 15 minutes in which to complete them. Calculators are not permitted. Simply circle your choice of answer using a pen or pencil.

Question 1

37 + ? = 95

A.	B.	C.	D.	E.
85	45	58	57	122

Question 2

86 − ? = 32

A.	B.	C.	D.	E.
54	45	108	118	68

Question 3

? + 104 = 210

A.	B.	C.	D.	E.
601	314	61	106	110

Question 4

109 × ? = 218

A.	B.	C.	D.	E.
1	109	12	10	2

Question 5

6 + 9 + 15 = 15 × ?

A.	B.	C.	D.	E.
15	2	3	4	5

Question 6

$(34 + 13) - 4 = ? + 3$

A.	B.	C.	D.	E.
7	47	51	40	37

Question 7

$35 \div ? = 10 + 7.5$

A.	B.	C.	D.	E.
2	10	4	1	17

Question 8

$7 \times ? = 28 \times 3$

A.	B.	C.	D.	E.
2	3	21	15	12

Question 9

$100 \div 4 = 67 - ?$

A.	B.	C.	D.	E.
42	24	57	333	2

Question 10

$32 \times 9 = 864 \div ?$

A.	B.	C.	D.	E.
288	3	882	4	None of these

Question II

Following the pattern shown in the number sequence below, what is the missing number?

9   18   ?   72   144   288

A.	B.	C.	D.	E.
27	36	49	21	63

Question 12

If you count from 1 to 100, how many 6s will you pass on the way?

A.	B.	C.	D.	E.
10	19	20	11	21

Question 13

50% of 350 equals?

A.	B.	C.	D.	E.
170	25	175	170	700

Question 14

75% of 1000 equals?

A.	B.	C.	D.	E.
75	0.75	75000	750	7.5

Question 15

40% of 40 equals?

A.	B.	C.	D.	E.
160	4	1600	1.6	16

Question 16

25% of 75 equals?

A.	B.	C.	D.	E.
18	18.75	18.25	25	17.25

Question 17

15% of 500 equals?

A.	B.	C.	D.	E.
75	50	0.75	0.505	750

Question 18

5% of 85 equals?

A.	B.	C.	D.	E.
4	80	4.25	0.85	89.25

Question 19

9876 – 6789 equals?

A.	B.	C.	D.	E.
3078	3085	783	3086	3087

Question 20

27 × 4 equals?

A	B.	C.	D.	E.
106	107	108	109	110

Question 21

96 ÷ 4 equals?

A.	B.	C.	D.	E.
22	23	24	25	26

Question 22

8765 – 876 equals?

A.	B.	C.	D.	E.
9887	7888	7890	7998	7889

Question 23

623 + 222 equals?

A.	B.	C.	D.	E.
840	845	740	745	940

Question 24

A rectangle has an area of 24 cm². The length of one side is 8 cm. What is the perimeter of the rectangle?

A.	B.	C.	D.	E.
22 inches	24 cm	18 cm	22 cm	18 inches

Question 25

A square has a perimeter of 36 cm. Its area is 81 cm². What is the length of one side?

A.	B.	C.	D.	E.
9 cm	18 cm	9 metres	18 metres	16 cm

Question 26

Which of the following is the same as 25/1000?

A.	B.	C.	D.	E.
0.25	0.025	0.0025	40	25000

Question 27

Is 33 divisible by 3?

A.	B.
Yes	No

Question 28

What is 49% of 1100?

A.	B.	C.	D.	E.
535	536	537	538	539

Question 29

One side of a rectangle is 12 cm. If the area of the rectangle is 84 cm^2, what is the length of the shorter side?

A.	B.	C.	D.	E.
5 cm	6 cm	7 cm	8 cm	9 cm

Question 30

A rectangle has an area of 8 cm^2. The length of one side is 2 cm. What is the perimeter?

A.	B.	C.	D.	E.
4 cm	6 cm	8 cm	10 cm	None of these

Now that you have completed the Practice Numeracy test work through your answers carefully before moving on to the next section of the BARB test.

Answers to the Practice Numeracy test

1.	C	11.	B	21.	C
2.	A	12.	C	22.	E
3.	D	13.	C	23.	B
4.	E	14.	D	24.	D
5.	B	15.	E	25.	A
6.	D	16.	B	26.	B
7.	A	17.	A	27.	A
8.	E	18.	C	28.	E
9.	A	19.	E	29.	C
10.	B	20.	C	30.	E

CHAPTER II
SELECTING THE ODD ONE OUT

As part of the BARB test you will be required to sit a Selecting the Odd One Out test. The requirement of this test is simply to select the odd one out from a group of words. Take a look at the following sample question.

Sample question I

Which of the following is the odd one out?

Ball   Footballer   Tree

The answer to this question is **Tree**. The reason is that Ball and Footballer are associated together, whereas Tree cannot be placed in the same category as the other two words, so therefore is the odd one out. You may find some words are the opposite of another one, which again is the association or connection. Here's another example.

Sample question 2

Which of the following is the odd one out?

Warm   Cold   Car

The odd one out in this example is **Car**. Warm is opposite to Cold, so therefore Car is the odd one out.

Now try the exercise on the following pages. Remember to read the questions carefully. When you sit the real test with the Army you may have to take the test on a computer as described earlier. An example of a question presented on a computer screen would be as follows:

Sky	Cloud	River

In this particular question **River** is the odd one out. Allow yourself 2 minutes only to answer as many questions as possible on the following exercise which contains 14 questions. Simply circle which word you believe is the odd one out. Once again the times provided in this sample test are different from the real test.

Selecting the Odd One Out: Exercise 1

Question 1

Bark	Sun	Tree

Question 2

Peanut	Mechanic	Spanner

Question 3

Hello	Goodbye	Running

Question 4

Plane	Ship	Centipede

Question 5

Kilo	Gram	Sugar

Question 6

Garage	Swing	Playground

Question 7

Poor	Rich	Grass

Question 8

You	Lady	Me

Question 9

Good	Table	Bad

Question 10

Little	Date	Large

Question II

Wet	Dry	Ear

Question I2

Old	Young	Light

Question I3

Day	Night	Road

Question I4

Forever	New	Fresh

Answers to Selecting the Odd One Out: Exercise 1

1. Sun		**8.** Lady	
2. Peanut		**9.** Table	
3. Running		**10.** Date	
4. Centipede		**11.** Ear	
5. Sugar		**12.** Light	
6. Garage		**13.** Road	
7. Grass		**14.** Forever	

Once you have checked all of your answers thoroughly move on to Exercise 2 on the following page. In this exercise there are 14 questions and you have 2 minutes in which to complete them.

Selecting the Odd One Out: Exercise 2

Question 1

| Wheel | Art | Painting |

Question 2

| Sunny | Grass | Raining |

Question 3

| Kitchen | Attic | Sea |

Question 4

| Pie | Soup | Gravel |

Question 5

| Bike | Farmer | Pigs |

Question 6

| Computer | Can | Drink |

Question 7

| Trousers | Shoes | Trainers |

Question 8

| Men | Women | Army |

Question 9

Horrible	Nice	Nasty

Question 10

Window	Brick	Cement

Question 11

Spoon	Red	Yellow

Question 12

Money	Car	Bank

Question 13

Cardboard	Queen	Plastic

Question 14

Fix	Wooden	Repair

Once you have completed Exercise 2 work through your answers correcting any that you get wrong; then move on to Exercise 3.

Answers to Selecting the Odd One Out: Exercise 2

1. Wheel
2. Grass
3. Sea
4. Gravel
5. Bike
6. Computer
7. Trainers
8. Army
9. Nice
10. Cement
11. Spoon
12. Car
13. Queen
14. Wooden

Selecting the Odd One Out: Exercise 3

Question 1

Baby	Daylight	Cot

Question 2

Hard	Firm	Soft

Question 3

Mortar	Sailing	Bricks

Question 4

Dream	Umpire	Cricket

Question 5

Repeat	Laces	Shoes

Question 6

Eat	Dine	Wrist

Question 7

Tree	Brakes	Car

Question 8

Telephone	Communicate	Bicycle

Question 9

Reach	Grab	Desire

Question 10

Leaf	Cow	Pony

Question 11

Moisturiser	Cream	Distance

Question 12

Road	Battle	Truck

Question 13

Midnight	Moon	Castle

Question 14

Shed	Baking	Food

Answers to Selecting the Odd One Out: Exercise 3

1. Daylight
2. Soft
3. Sailing
4. Dream
5. Repeat
6. Wrist
7. Plate

8. Bicycle
9. Desire
10. Leaf
11. Distance
12. Battle
13. Castle
14. Shed

Once you have checked all of your answers thoroughly move on to the next section of the BARB test which is the Symbol Rotation test.

CHAPTER 12
THE SYMBOL ROTATION TEST

During the BARB test you will be required to sit the Symbol Rotation test. The requirement of this test is to identify which symbols match after rotation.

Take a look at the following two pairs of letters:

You will see that both pairs of letters are the *same*. The only difference is that the letters have each been rotated. Now take a look at the next two pairs of letters:

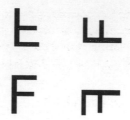

You will see that if each letter on the top row is rotated through all angles, it is impossible to match it up with the bottom letter directly below it. Therefore the letters are said to be a *mirror* image of each other.

During the Symbol Rotation test you will be required to identify how many pairs of symbols are matching. You will have to rotate the letters/symbols in your mind and decide how many of the pairs that are presented in front of you actually match. Take a look at the following three pairs of letters and decide how many are matching:

Sample question I

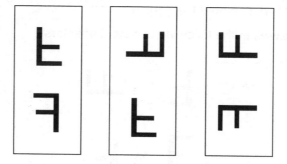

You will see that the letters in the first two boxes can be rotated round to match. The pair in the third box however cannot be rotated to match. Therefore there are *two* pairs in this sequence that are identical.

Now try the exercise on the following pages. Your task is to identify how many pairs of letters match in each sequence.

You have 5 minutes to complete the exercise of 15 questions. Simply circle which answer is correct in the box beneath each question. The times provided in the following sample exercises are not the same as for the real test.

Symbol Rotation test: Exercise 1

Question 1

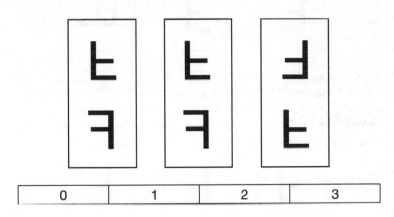

Question 2

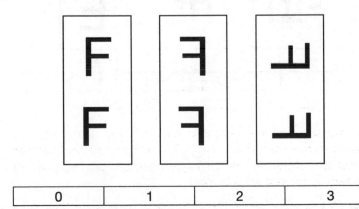

Question 3

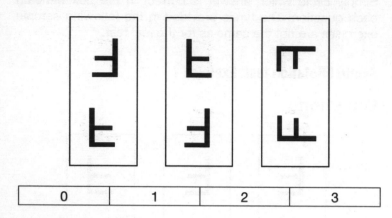

| 0 | 1 | 2 | 3 |

Question 4

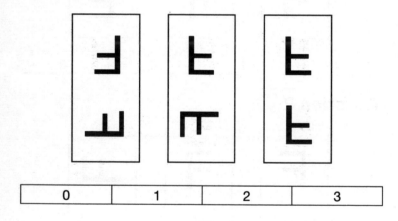

| 0 | 1 | 2 | 3 |

Question 5

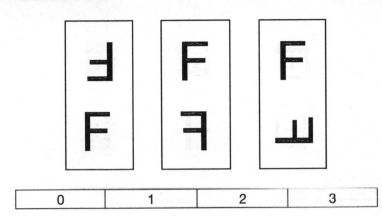

| 0 | 1 | 2 | 3 |

Question 6

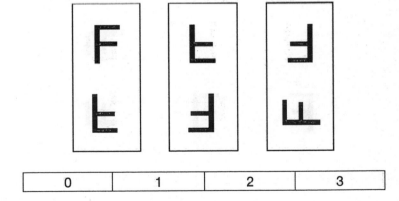

| 0 | 1 | 2 | 3 |

Question 7

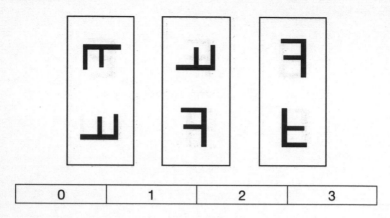

| 0 | 1 | 2 | 3 |

Question 8

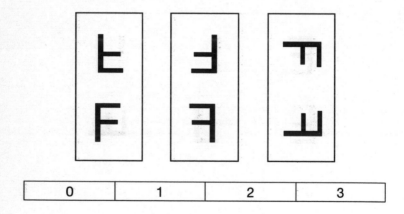

| 0 | 1 | 2 | 3 |

Question 9

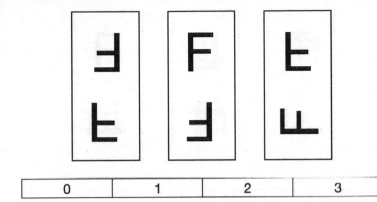

| 0 | 1 | 2 | 3 |

Question 10

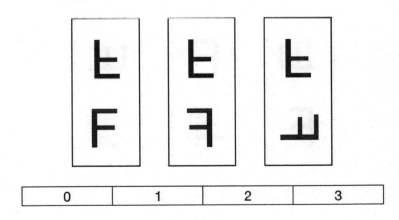

| 0 | 1 | 2 | 3 |

Question II

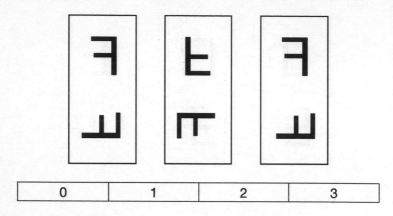

| 0 | 1 | 2 | 3 |

Question 12

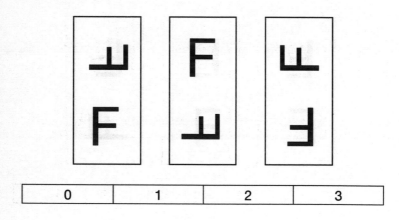

| 0 | 1 | 2 | 3 |

Question 13

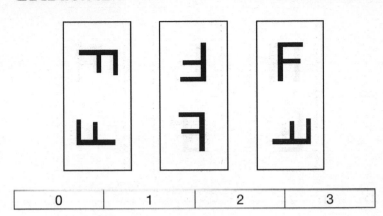

| 0 | 1 | 2 | 3 |

Question 14

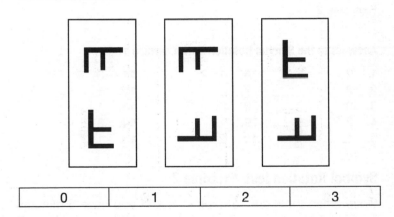

| 0 | 1 | 2 | 3 |

Question 15

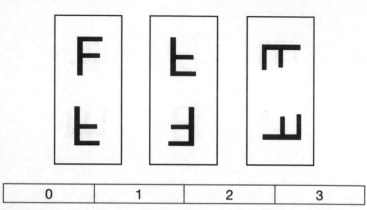

| 0 | 1 | 2 | 3 |

Now that you have completed the exercise take the time to check over your answers carefully before moving on to Exercise 2.

Answers to the Symbol Rotation test: Exercise 1

1. 2		**6.** 1		**11.** 3
2. 3		**7.** 3		**12.** 1
3. 0		**8.** 0		**13.** 1
4. 2		**9.** 1		**14.** 3
5. 1		**10.** 2		**15.** 1

Symbol Rotation test: Exercise 2

Once again there are 15 questions and you have 5 minutes to work through them. Circle the correct answer in the box provided.

Question 1

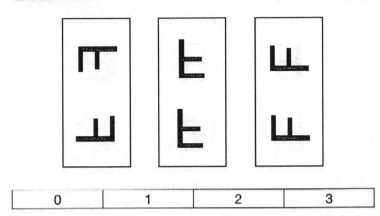

0	1	2	3

Question 2

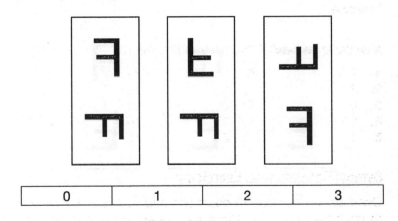

0	1	2	3

Question 3

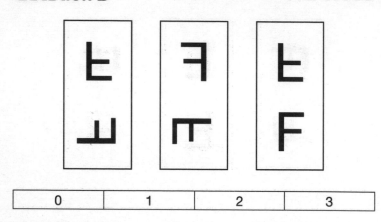

| 0 | 1 | 2 | 3 |

Question 4

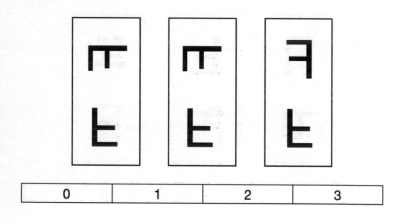

| 0 | 1 | 2 | 3 |

Question 5

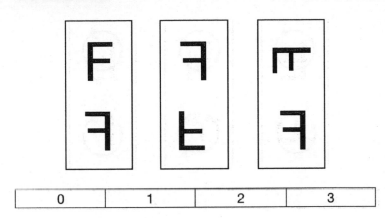

| 0 | 1 | 2 | 3 |

Question 6

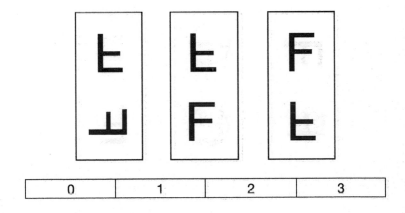

| 0 | 1 | 2 | 3 |

Question 7

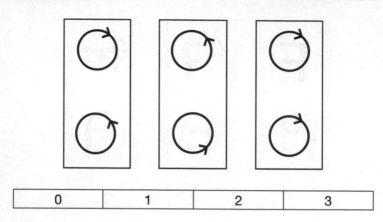

| 0 | 1 | 2 | 3 |

Question 8

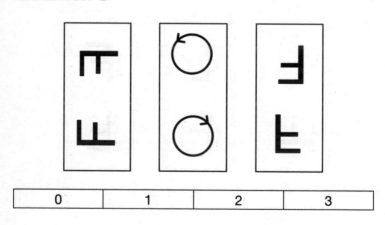

| 0 | 1 | 2 | 3 |

Question 9

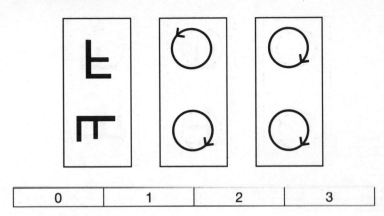

| 0 | 1 | 2 | 3 |

Question 10

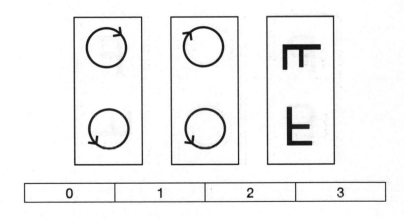

| 0 | 1 | 2 | 3 |

Question 11

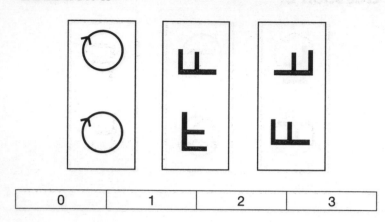

0	1	2	3

Question 12

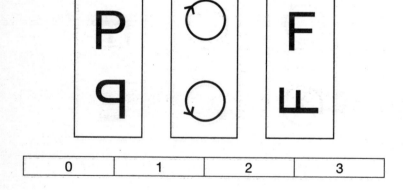

0	1	2	3

Question 13

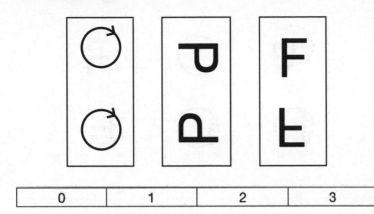

| 0 | 1 | 2 | 3 |

Question 14

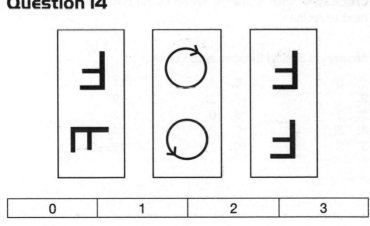

| 0 | 1 | 2 | 3 |

Question 15

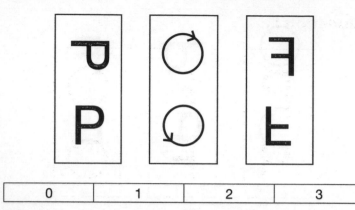

| 0 | 1 | 2 | 3 |

Now that you have completed the exercise take the time to check over your answers carefully before moving onto the next exercise.

Answers to Symbol Rotation test: Exercise 2

1.	3	**6.**	1	**11.**	1
2.	1	**7.**	2	**12.**	1
3.	2	**8.**	0	**13.**	2
4.	3	**9.**	2	**14.**	1
5.	2	**10.**	1	**15.**	2

Symbol Rotation test: Exercise 3

Question 1

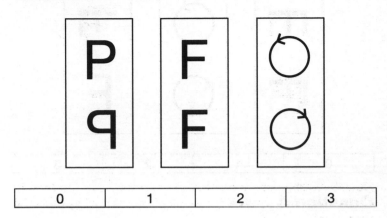

| 0 | 1 | 2 | 3 |

Question 2

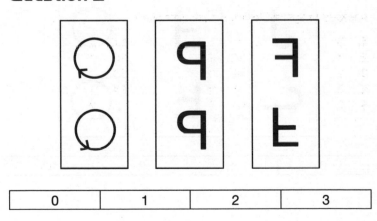

| 0 | 1 | 2 | 3 |

Question 3

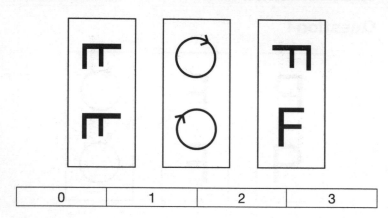

0	1	2	3

Question 4

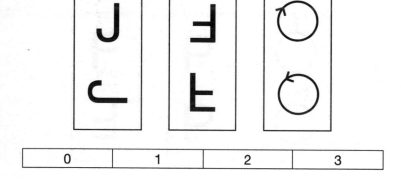

0	1	2	3

Question 5

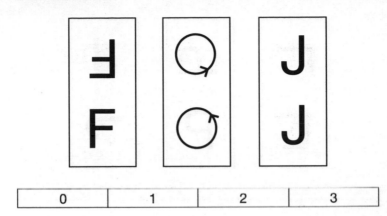

0	1	2	3

Question 6

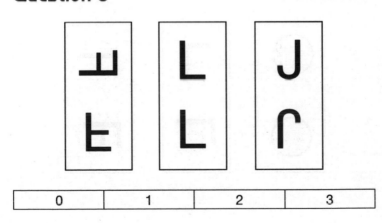

0	1	2	3

Question 7

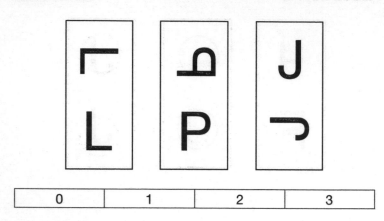

| 0 | 1 | 2 | 3 |

Question 8

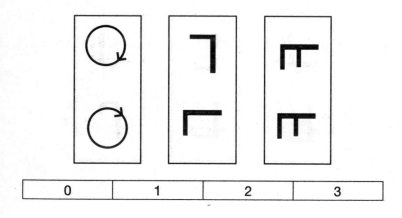

| 0 | 1 | 2 | 3 |

Question 9

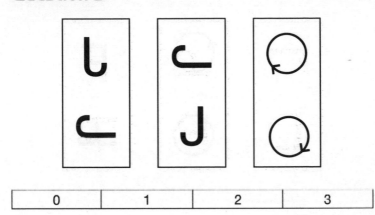

| 0 | 1 | 2 | 3 |

Question 10

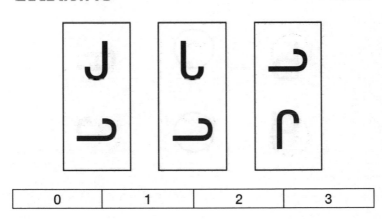

| 0 | 1 | 2 | 3 |

Question 11

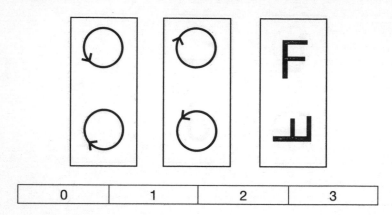

0	1	2	3

Question 12

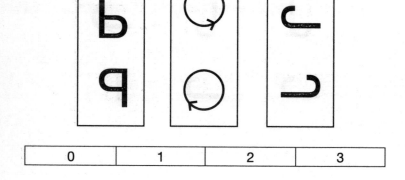

0	1	2	3

Question 13

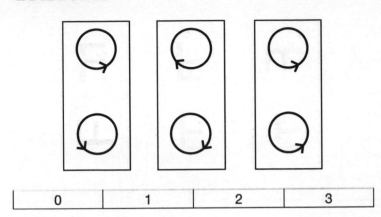

| 0 | 1 | 2 | 3 |

Question 14

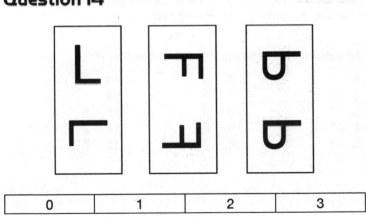

| 0 | 1 | 2 | 3 |

Question 15

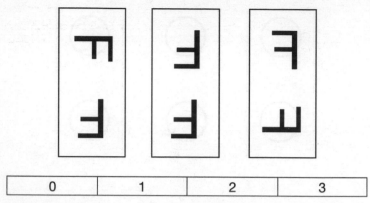

0	1	2	3

Now that you have completed the exercise take the time to check over your answers carefully before moving on to the final tips for passing the BARB test.

Answers to Symbol Rotation test: Exercise 3

1. 1	**6.** 3	**11.** 0
2. 2	**7.** 2	**12.** 1
3. 3	**8.** 3	**13.** 3
4. 1	**9.** 2	**14.** 2
5. 3	**10.** 1	**15.** 3

CHAPTER 13
FINAL TIPS FOR PASSING THE BARB TEST

Success at the BARB test will be very much dependent on how much and the type of preparation you carry out. Don't forget to make your preparation deliberate by carrying out plenty of repetitive practice in your weakness areas. For example, if you feel that you are poor at the Distance Number test then get yourself of copy of a numerical reasoning test booklet and work hard at the questions. If you are really worried about your testing ability then consider obtaining a personal tutor to help you. Your practice should be over a prolonged period of time, not by cramming the night before your test. Little and often is the key to success.

Take care of what you eat and drink in the build up to the test. Avoid alcohol and caffeine in the few days leading up to the test and get plenty of rest. You will want to be at your best during the test and all of these small tips will help you to improve on your scores.

THE ARMY DEVELOPMENT AND SELECTION CENTRE

CHAPTER 14
PREPARING FOR ADSC ASSESSMENT

This section contains useful information that will help you to prepare for the Army Development and Selection Centre (ADSC) assessment. This stage comes after your initial application and BARB test results and the decision to recommend you for ADSC will rest with your Armed Forces Careers Officer.

The purpose of the ADSC is to assess whether you are suitable to join the Army but to also see whether the Army is suitable for you. During the two-day ADSC you will get to speak to serving recruits and you will have the opportunity to get a feel for life within the Army. Preparation for ADSC should start as soon as you have taken the BARB test and it should be as focused as the previous stages. You will want to be at your best during ADSC to gain high scores. It is crucial that you give 100 per cent to everything during the ADSC and that you also create the right impression. The Army will pay for your travel, usually by train, to attend ADSC.

You should get to the ADSC in plenty of time. The last thing you need is to arrive late as this will get you off on the wrong

foot. Also attend in a smart formal outfit such as a suit, shirt and tie or smart jacket and skirt or trousers. The majority of candidates will arrive in tracksuits or jeans and trainers. After speaking to serving Army Officers during the research for this book it was made perfectly clear that they would prefer to see candidates arrive at ADSC smartly dressed. Make sure your shoes are clean and tidy and remember to take everything with you that is required, including relevant documentation.

About the ADSC

There are a number of ADSCs across the country where a total of 10,000 people apply in any one year. The two-day ADSC is designed to assess whether you are suitable for Army life, whether Army life is suitable for you, and also what jobs you may be suited to if you successfully pass the entire selection process. The entrance level fitness test involves a series of strength tests, fitness tests and a mile-and-a-half run.

The medical

One of the very first stages of ADSC is the medical. The medical is a thorough examination that includes various forms to fill and assessments. You will need to be passed fit by the Army doctor in order to progress to the next stage of the ADSC. If the Army is unsure about a certain aspect of your health then it may refer you to a specialist or another doctor for further checks.

The ice breaker/initial presentation

During the ADSC you will be required to carry out a two-minute 'ice breaker' presentation to the rest of the group. This will usually follow the initial medical. The ice breaker is designed to do exactly what it says – break the ice and the nervousness that is all part of ADSC. You will usually be required to talk about a number of topics relating to yourself such as:

- name
- age
- where you are from
- who your family consists of
- your hobbies and general interests
- the reasons why you have chosen your regiment/corps
- something interesting about you or your most memorable moment
- your ambitions in life
- what you can offer the Army
- what you are good at and what you are not so good at.

You need to practise carrying out a mini-presentation on the above subject areas before you attend the ADSC. Your audience could be your family or a small group of friends. This will help reduce any nerves you may have whilst speaking in front of a group of people. When giving your presentation at the ADSC make sure you stand up straight at all times and speak confidently, clearly and concisely. Your ability to communicate with confidence is important and the only way to achieve confidence is through practice. Give your presentation to everybody in the room instead of looking at just one person. Try to make your presentation interesting and also try to throw in something which is humorous as this will help to break the ice. When speaking about your hobbies and interests make sure you demonstrate that you are an active person who participates in team sports and activities.

Things *not* to say during your presentation include:

- that you have done little or no preparation for ADSC
- you don't like being told what to do by others
- you don't like your job or school

- you are not very active or physically fit
- you are not confident of passing ADSC.

Gym tests and the 1.5-mile run

During the ADSC you will be required to carry out a number of fitness tests in the gym and also a 'best effort' 1.5-mile run. Before you attend the ADSC you should aim to comfortably achieve 50 press-ups within 2 minutes, and 50 sit-ups in 2 minutes. Your 'how to get soldier fit' guide is an excellent resource in helping your prepare for both of these. You may not have to carry out a sit-up or press-up test during the ADSC but you'll certainly be doing lots of them during the evening gym session. I would also recommend that you carry out a form of 'step-up' exercise. The Chester step test is a great way to improve your step-up performance and this can be obtained through the website www.how2become.co.uk.

During the evening gym session, which will last for approximately 45 minutes, you will be grouped with other candidates. During a set period of time you will be required to carry out basic repetitive exercises such as step-ups, press-ups or sit-ups whilst each member of the group runs backwards and forwards between two set points. You will be required to give 100 per cent during these tests so lots of preparation beforehand will work to improve your scores greatly.

As part of the ADSC you will also be required to carry out a 1.5-mile run which should be your best effort. This test always takes place outdoors and it is carried out on an even surface. To begin with, you will carry out a half-mile warm up before conducting the actual test. The official army standard requires you to complete the distance in 14 minutes (14 minutes and 30 seconds for juniors). It is very important that you can easily achieve the right minimum standard before you attend the ADSC for a very good reason. It is a well-known fact that those applicants who complete the 1.5-mile

run in over 14 minutes are far more likely to pick up an injury during training than those applicants who can do the run in 12 minutes or under. Therefore it is important that you can complete the run in less than 14 minutes before you attend ADSC!

Note that whilst the minimum standard is 14 minutes, there are varying standards set for the different sections of the Army, depending on which one you are applying for.

The strength tests

The good thing about the strength tests is that if you are fairly poor at one of them it does not necessarily mean you fail. There are five tests in all that you must complete. Once you have completed the tests your results will be calculated. The Army will also use your height and weight as an assessable factor when determining your strength. If you score poorly on the strength tests then this could mean that you are not suitable for certain jobs in the Army. An example of this could be building bridges in the Royal Engineers.

Pull-ups or heaves come first. You will be required to cling to a bar above your head and attempt to lift yourself up to meet it. You should be capable of carrying out ten heaves before you attend ADSC. Whilst this is not essential it will allow you to impress the gym staff and assessors. The tests of back extension, static lift and dynamic lift strength all necessitate standing on pieces of equipment while pulling or pushing weights, and holding the position for a set period of time. You will find that a number of these tests are carried out on various machines in the gym. These machines are used to measure your ability to lift weights that are firmly attached to immovable objects. It is the amount of force that you apply to the load cell that is important as this is recorded through a digital reading which is in kilograms (kg) of force.

Finally, you will head outside for the jerry can carrying assessment. The objective is to see how far you can carry

one jerry can in each hand without putting them down. Each jerry can will weigh 20 kgs.

The Information Retention test

During the ADSC you may be required to sit a form of Information Retention test. This will be based on an item of military equipment. One of the more common types of test used at the ADSC is the grenade test. The test requires you to listen to a lesson which is based on a specific hand grenade that is used by the Army. During the lesson it is important to listen carefully and absorb the information that is being provided. Once the lesson is complete you will be required to take a test.

Here are some of the most common questions that are used during the test. *Important note*: the following questions and answers are samples only and should not be relied upon to be the exact questions you will get asked during your test. The type of grenade used during the test will vary.

Sample question

What is the name of the grenade?

Sample answer

L110A1 or L109A1.

Sample question

What colour is the grenade?

Sample answer

L110A1 is dark blue with white stencilling. L109A1 is deep bronze green.

Sample question

What does 'inert' mean?

Sample answer

The grenade is 'live' but without the explosive device.

Sample question

What does 'HE' stand for?

Sample answer

High Explosion.

Sample question

What is the range of the grenade?

Sample answer

20 metres if the enemy is unprotected and 5 metres if the enemy is protected.

The Technical Selection test

The Technical Selection test (TST) is only for candidates who are applying to join specific branches and trades such as the Royal Engineers, Royal Signals, Royal Electrical and Mechanical Engineers, or the Royal Logistic Corps as an Ammunition Technician. Some other candidates may also be nominated to take the Technical Selection test depending on their job choices and qualifications. If the TST applies to you then I would recommend that you spend plenty of time improving your ability to work with numerical information and data prior to attending the ADSC. The type of questions that are normally used during the TST can include interpretation of

graphical data, division, subtraction, multiplication, addition, percentages, metric unit conversion, ratios, percentages, fractions, averages, volumes, equations and other similar mathematical calculations. One of the most useful resources to obtain for the Technical Selection test is a GCSE level maths book.

The team tasks

During the ADSC you will be required to carry out a number of team tasks which basically entail moving an item of equipment from A to B.

The priority for you as a candidate is to get involved, work as an effective team member, communicate with your colleagues and provide support and encouragement at every opportunity. It is essential that you get involved as those people who stand in the background hoping that they won't get noticed will fail. At the start of the team tasks the ADSC staff will provide you with a brief. Make sure you pay attention and listen to what is required. If you don't listen then you will not be able to complete the task. Try to come up with suitable ideas on how to solve the task. Even if you think your ideas may not work it is far better to participate than to say nothing.

Advice for working effectively as a member of a team during the ADSC

Having the ability to work as part of a team is essential to your career within the Army and you will need to demonstrate this ability during the ADSC. Working as a team does not involve being an individual who is only interested in his or her performance. It is the team's overall performance which should be the focus of attention. There are many different qualities that you'll require in order to become an effective team member.

Working in teams can be very rewarding, but at times it can be difficult and downright frustrating. If there are poor

communicators on your team, you may often feel left in the dark, confused or misunderstood. To create a successful team, effective communication methods are necessary for both team members and leaders. For example, during the team tasks that form part of the ADSC you will need to communicate with the other team members when discussing the task and whilst providing them with support and encouragement.

In addition to the team tasks there is a strong possibility that you will be asked questions relating to your ability to work as an effective team member during your interview with the Army Development and Selection Officer (ADSO). After all, it is teamwork that makes the Army operate as effectively as it does. Without it, it would not function.

A team's success or failure will be determined by the team's achievements, not your own. Whilst it is good to demonstrate that you can lead a team or show initiative and come up with strong solutions, it is the ability of team members to work together to achieve a goal that will be fundamental to the team's success. Everybody within a team has a role to play and some people will be better at doing specific tasks than others.

During the ADSC you will be given a set amount of time to discuss how you will carry out a specific task as part of the assessment. This time should be used to work out an effective plan and find out who is good at doing what. During this stage you will need to be vocal and come up with possible solutions to the task that is presented. If you stand in the background and let the others get on with it then you will score poorly. Even if you think your solutions are not very effective still put them forward.

Whatever happens, when working as part of a team be motivated and determined to succeed!

It is also a good idea to shout words of encouragement to other team members during the ADSC team tasks and look

out for those people who may be finding tasks difficult. Offer to help them out and provide them with support if required. Keep remembering that you are part of a team and not an individual whose aim is solely to impress.

When working as a team it is important to listen and respect other people's contributions, even though you may think that they are wrong or your idea is better than theirs. Make sure that everyone is involved when working as part of a team and if you see other people struggling or not contributing then try to involve them in some way.

The ADSC interview

During the ADSC you will be required to sit an interview with the ADSO that is designed to assess your motivation and suitability for joining the Army. Information relating to this interview, including sample questions and responses, is contained within earlier chapters of this book.

Tips for passing the ADSC

- Arrive early and wear a formal outfit,

- Make sure you pack everything that you are required to take with you and double check everything.

- Do not put your hands in your pockets at any time during your stay at the ADSC.

- Do not fold your arms or slouch.

- Make sure you listen very careful to each brief and concentrate at all times. The recruitment staff will ask you questions relating to the information they give you throughout the ADSC.

- During the team tasks ensure you get involved. Do not stay in the background but instead work as part of a team. Encourage others and support each member

---

of your team. If you fail to get involved or work as an effective team member then it is likely that you will fail the ADSC assessment.

- Leave all forms of jewellery at home otherwise you'll be required to take it off as soon as you arrive.

- During every assessment and test you must give 100 per cent effort. Even if you are finding it difficult, keep going.

- Before you attend the ADSC try practising an ice breaker. This effectively means standing up in front of a group of people and introducing yourself.

- Call the Officers 'Sir' or 'Ma'am' or as otherwise directed.

- Even though the ADSO interview is relatively informal, you must still create the right impression. Concentrate on your interview technique, sit upright in the chair, do not slouch and address the selection officer as 'Sir' or 'Ma'am'.

FREE BONUS GUIDE –
HOW TO GET SOLDIER FIT

Introduction

Welcome to your 'How to get Soldier Fit' information guide. Within this guide I have provided you with a number of exercises and tips that will assist you during your preparation for the Army selection process. Each exercise has been designed to improve your performance in each of the testing areas during the Army Development and Selection Centre (ADSC) assessment.

The physical tests that you will be required to undertake during the ADSC will require a combination of aerobic fitness, upper body strength and lower body strength. Your fitness preparation should start well before you attend the ADSC. In my experience, the majority of candidates wait until they receive their ADSC date before embarking on a fitness programme. In my view, this is setting out on the route to failure. As soon as you finish reading this book get started on your fitness preparation. Chapter 3 contains a sample

weekly timetable which involved both academic and fitness preparation. By adding a structured 'routine' to your training programme and also varying the type of preparatory work that you carry out you will be maintaining higher levels of motivation and concentration. If you work solely on one area of preparation, for example BARB test practice, you will soon become tired and bored. However, if you mix up your preparation with a specifically targeted physical fitness programme then the chances of you becoming demotivated will greatly decline.

In addition to improving your physical fitness levels keep an eye on your diet and eat healthy foods whilst drinking plenty of water. This will all go a long way to helping you improve your general well-being and concentration levels.

As with any form of exercise you should consult your doctor first.

Warning – Ensure you take advice from a competent fitness trainer in relation to the correct execution of press-up exercises and other exercises contained within this guide. You may find that the techniques for carrying out the exercises in this guide differ from the requirements of the British Army.

Planning your workouts and preparing for the Army Fitness tests

The key to a successful fitness preparation strategy is variety and continuous improvement. When you start your fitness programme you should be highly motivated. The hard part will come a couple of weeks into your programme when your rate of improvement decreases. It is at this point that you must vary your exercise routine in order to ensure that you stay on the right track and don't lose interest. The reason why most people give up on their fitness regime is mainly owing to a lack of proper preparation. Throughout this book the word 'preparation' has been integral, and the same word

applies when preparing for the fitness tests. Preparation is key to your success and it is essential that you plan your workouts effectively.

As you are fully aware, soldiers are extremely fit people and they take a great pride in their appearance. Some of them will be keen runners whilst others will be keen weight trainers. In the build-up to the ADSC concentrate on specific exercises that will allow you to pass the tests with ease. These exercises may not be what you expect, simply because they are not based around lifting heavy weights or running extreme marathon distances!

Read on for some great ways not only pass to the ADSC fitness tests, but also to stay soldier fit all year round.

Get an assessment before you start training

The first step is to conduct a 'self-fitness test'. This should involve the following four areas:

1. a 1.5-mile run in the fastest time possible

2. as many sit-ups as possible in 2 minutes

3. as many press-ups as possible in 2 minutes

4. as many pull-ups or heaves as possible without stopping.

The first three tests will be easy to perform as you do not require a gym or gym equipment to carry them out. However, the pull-ups are a different matter. If possible, get yourself a pull-up bar of the type that fits within a doorway. You should be able to find a suitable, cheap one via an online sports website or get one second hand. The investment will be worthwhile. However, make sure it conforms to the relevant safety standards and that it can easily support your weight. Also ensure you get permission from the owner of the house before you start to install your pull-up bar!

Once you have done all four of these tests you should write down your results and keep them somewhere safe. After two

weeks of following your new fitness regime, do all four tests again and check your results against the previous week's results. This is a great way to monitor your performance and progress and it will also keep you motivated and focused on your goals.

Keep a check on what you eat and drink

Before we get started with stretching and targeted exercises write down everything you eat and drink for a whole week. You must include tea, water, milk, biscuits and anything and everything that you ingest. You will soon begin to realise how much you are eating and will notice areas in which you can make some changes. For example, if you are taking sugar with your tea then why not try reducing it or giving it up altogether. If you do then you will soon notice the difference. Because you are about to embark on a rigorous fitness training regime you will need to fill your body with the right type of fuel. This includes both food and drink. Let's get one thing straight from the offset, if you fill your body with rubbish then your fitness performance is likely to be on a par with rubbish. Fill it with the right nutrients and vitamins and you will perform far more effectively. When I was 26 years old I decided to do my own version of the ironman challenge for a local charity. I swam 2 miles, then I ran a marathon, before finally completing a 120-mile cycle ride, all one after the other! I managed to raise over £10,000 for a children's hospice in Kent. In the six months prior to the challenge I trained very hard, but I also put just as much effort into what I ate and drank. This would prove crucial to my success in achieving the challenge.

During your fitness training programme I would recommend you totally avoid the high calorie foods that lack the right level of nutrients such as chips, burgers, chocolates, sweets, fizzy drinks and alcohol, etc. Instead, replace them with fruit, cereals, vegetables, pasta, rice, chicken and fish. You also need to make sure you drink plenty of water throughout the day in order to keep yourself fully hydrated. This will help to

keep your concentration levels up, which you will need for the BARB test and the Technical Selection tests (if applicable). Many people who keep fit use vitamin supplements and energy enhancing drinks. Generally, you don't need any of these providing you drink plenty of water and you stick to a balanced diet that includes the right vitamins and nutrients. Spend your hard earned money on something else instead of buying supplements, powders and energy drinks.

It is important that you start to look for opportunities to improve your fitness and well-being right from the offset. These areas are what I call 'easy wins'.

You don't need to lift heavy weights in order to pass the ADSC

When I applied to join the Fire Service the physical tests were rigorous, demanding and extremely difficult to pass. As part of the assessment I was required to bench press 50 kg, 20 times within 60 seconds. You do *not* have to lift heavy weights in order to pass the ADSC fitness tests. You will be better off including some form of light weight work which is specifically targeted at increasing stamina, strength and endurance. Instead of performing bench presses at the gym, replace them with press-ups. Instead of performing heavy lateral pull-down exercises replace them with pull-ups, which only utilise your own body weight.

There are some more great exercises contained within this guide and most of them can be carried out without the need to attend a gym.

One step at a time

Only you will know how fit you are. First of all write down the areas that you believe or feel you need to improve on. For example, if you feel that you need to work on your upper body strength then pick out exercises from this guide that will work on that area. The majority of people who are getting ready for ADSC will be relatively weak at pull-ups and this is

an area that you should work hard on to improve. Make sure you can do at least ten pull-ups before you attend ADSC. Your AFCO adviser will probably still recommend you for ADSC if you can only do less than ten, but this should still be your minimum target.

The key to making improvements is to do it gradually, and one step at a time. Try to set yourself small goals. When you carry out your initial 'self-fitness test' you may find that you can only achieve a few press-ups, sit-ups and pull-ups. Instead of focusing on the magic target of 50 press-ups within 2 minutes, break down your goals into easy-to-achieve stepping stones. For example, by the end of the first week aim to achieve an additional ten press-ups and sit-ups. Then, add another ten to the second week's target and so on. One of the biggest problems that many people encounter when starting a fitness regime is that they become bored very quickly. This then leads to a lack of motivation and desire, and soon the fitness programme stops. Change your exercise routine often in order to maintain your interest levels. Instead of running every day, try swimming or indoor rowing. This will keep your interest and motivational levels high and it will also work other muscle groups that running does not focus on.

Stretching

How many people stretch before carrying out any form of exercise? Very few is the correct answer. Not only is it irresponsible but it is also placing yourself at high risk from injury. The last thing you need is an injury prior to ADSC, especially after the amount of hard work you have put in to ensure you pass. Before I commence with the exercises let's take a look at a few warm-up stretches. Make sure you stretch fully before carrying out any exercises. You want your Army career to be a long one and that means looking after yourself, including stretching! It is also very important to check with your GP that you are medically fit to carry out any form of physical exercise.

The warm-up calf stretch

To perform this stretch effectively you should first of all start off by facing a wall whilst standing upright. Your right foot should be close to the wall and your right knee bent. Now place your hands flat against the wall and at a height that is level with your shoulders. Stretch your left leg far out behind you without lifting your toes and heel off the floor, and lean towards the wall.

Once you have performed this stretch for 25 seconds switch legs and carry out the same procedure for the left leg. As with all exercises contained within this guide, stop if you feel any pain or discomfort.

Stretching the shoulder muscles

To begin with, stand with your feet slightly apart and with your knees only slightly bent. Now hold your arms right out in front of you and with your palms facing away from you with your fingers pointing skywards. Now place your right palm on the back of your left hand and use it to push the left hand further away from you. If you are performing this exercise correctly then you will feel the muscles in your shoulder stretching. Hold for 10 seconds before switching sides.

Stretching the quad muscles (front of the thigh)

Before you carry out any form of running it is imperative that you stretch your leg muscles. During the ADSC fitness tests the instructors should take you through a series of warm-up exercises which will include stretching the quad muscles. To begin with, stand with your left hand pressed against a wall or firm surface. Bend your left knee slightly and bring your right heel up to your bottom whilst grasping your foot with your right hand (see diagram opposite). Your back should be straight and your shoulders, hips and knees should all be in line at all times during the exercise. Hold for 25 seconds before switching legs.

Stretching the hamstring muscles (back of the thigh)

It is very easy to injure your hamstring muscles as a soldier especially with all of the running you'll be doing during your career. Therefore you must get into the routine of stretching out the hamstring muscles before every training session.

To perform this exercise correctly, stand up straight and place your right foot onto a table or other firm surface so that your leg is almost parallel to the floor. Keep your left leg straight and your foot at a right angle to your leg. Start to slowly move your hands down your right leg towards your ankle until you feel tension on the underside of your thigh. When you feel this tension you know that you are starting to stretch the hamstring muscles. Hold for 25 seconds before switching legs.

I have only covered a small number of stretching exercises within this section; however, it is crucial that you stretch out fully in all areas before carrying out any of the following exercises. Remember to obtain professional advice before carrying out any type of exercise.

Running

One of the great ways to prepare for the ADSC fitness tests is to embark on a structured running programme. You do not need to run extreme long distances in order to gain massively from this type of exercise. As part of the ADSC fitness tests you will be required to run 1.5-miles in under 14 minutes. For some regiments such as the Parachute Regiment you will need to do this in approximately 9 minutes. Don't settle for the minimum standard but instead keep pushing yourself and improving your stamina/fitness levels.

Towards the end of this guide I have provided you with a number of weekly training programmes for you to follow. These incorporate running and series of combined exercises that will help you to prepare for the ADSC.

Tips for running

- As with any exercise you should consult a doctor before taking part to make sure that you are medically fit.

- It is certainly worth investing in a pair of comfortable running shoes that serve the purpose of your intended training programme. Your local sports shop will be able to advise you on the type that is best for you. You don't have to spend a fortune to buy a good pair of running shoes.

- It is a good idea to invest in a 'high visibility' jacket or coat so that you can be seen by fast-moving traffic if you intend to run on or near the road.

- Make sure you carry out at least 5 whole minutes of stretching exercises not only before but also after your running programme. This can help to prevent injury.

- Whilst you shouldn't run on a full stomach, it is also not good to run on an empty one either. An excellent food to eat approximately 30 minutes before a run is a banana. This is great for giving you sustained energy.

- Drink plenty of water throughout the day, at least 1.5 litres each day in total. This will keep you hydrated and help to prevent muscle cramp.

- Don't overdo it. If you feel any pain or discomfort then stop and seek medical advice.

- When preparing for the Army selection process, use your exercise time as a break from your studies. For example, if you have been practising numerical reasoning tests for an hour, why not take a break and go running? When you return from your run you can then concentrate on your studies feeling refreshed.

Exercises that will improve your ability to pass the Army Fitness tests

Press-ups

Whilst running is a great way to improve your overall fitness, you will also need to carry out exercises that improve your

upper body strength. These exercises will help you to pass the Army fitness tests where you need to carry heavy items of equipment such as jerry cans over a long distance.

The great thing about press-ups is that you don't have to attend a gym to perform them. However, you must ensure that you can do them correctly or you may get injured. You only need to spend 5 minutes every day on press-ups, possibly after you go running or even before if you prefer. If you are not used to doing press-ups then start slowly and aim to carry out at least ten.

Even if you struggle to do just ten, you will soon find that after a few days' practice at these you will be up to 20+.

- **Step 1** – To begin with, lie on a mat or even surface. Your hands should be shoulder width apart and fully extend the arms.

- **Step 2** – Gradually lower your body until the elbows reach a 90-degree angle. Do not rush the movement as you may cause injury.

- **Step 3** – Once your elbows reach 90° slowly return to the starting position with your arms fully extended.

The press-up action should be a continuous movement with no rest. However, it is important that the exercise is as smooth as possible and there should be no jolting or sudden movements. Try to complete as many press-ups as possible and always keep a record of how many you do. This will keep your focus and also maintain your motivation levels.

Sit-ups

Sit-ups are great for building the core stomach muscles. Strong abdominal muscles are important for lifting items of equipment, something which is integral to the role of a soldier. If you are applying to join regiments such as the Royal Engineers where lifting and carrying are a core part of the role then you will need to have very good all-round stamina and strength.

At the commencement of the exercise lie flat on your back with your knees bent at a 45° angle and with your feet together. Your hands can either be crossed on your chest, by your sides, or cupped behind your ears as shown here.

Without moving your lower body, curl your upper torso upwards and in towards your knees, until your shoulder blades are as high off the ground as possible. As you reach the highest point, tighten your abdominal muscles for a brief second. This will allow you to get the most out of the exercise. Now slowly start to lower yourself back to the starting position. You should be aiming to work up to at least 50 effective sit-ups within a 2-minute period. You will be amazed at how quickly this can be achieved and you will begin to notice your stomach muscles toning.

Pull-ups or heaves

As part of the ADSC you will be required to carry out a 'heaves' test. This test will require you to hang from a static

bar and pull yourself up to the top so that you head is over the bar before lowering yourself back down gradually. You will be required to carry out as many as possible within a dedicated timeframe. The unfortunate thing about this type of exercise is you will probably need to attend a gym in order to carry them out. Having said that, there are a number of different types of 'pull-up bars' available to buy on the market that can easily and safely be fitted to a doorway at home. If you choose to purchase one of these items first make sure that it conforms to the relevant safety standards.

Pull-ups or heaves are very effective at increasing upper body strength. If you have access to a gym then these can be practised on a 'lateral pull-down' machine. Consult your gym member of staff to ask about these exercises.

Pull-ups should be performed by firmly grasping a sturdy and solid bar. Before you grasp the bar make sure it is safe. Your hands should be roughly shoulder width apart. Straighten your arms so that your body hangs loose. You will feel your lateral muscles and biceps stretching as you hang in the air. This is the starting position for the lateral pull-up exercise.

Next, pull yourself upwards to the point where your chest is almost touching the bar and your chin is actually over the bar. Whilst pulling upwards, focus on keeping your body straight without any arching or swinging as this can result in injury. Once your chin is over the bar, you can lower yourself back down to the initial starting position. Repeat the exercise ten times.

Squats

Squats are a great exercise for working the leg and bottom muscles. They are the perfect exercise in your preparation for Army strength tests.

At the start of the exercise, stand up straight with your arms at your sides. Concentrate on keeping your feet shoulder width apart and your head up. Do not look down at any point during the exercise. You will see from the diagram (over page) that the woman has her lower back slightly arched. She is also holding light weights which can add to the intensity of the exercise.

Now start to very slowly bend your knees while pushing your bottom out as though you are about to sit down on a chair. Keep lowering yourself until your thighs reach past the 90° point. Make sure your weight is on your heels so that your knees do not extend over your toes. At this point you may want to tighten your thighs and buttocks to intensify the exercise.

As you come back up to a standing position, push down through your heels, which will allow you to maintain your balance. Repeat the exercise 15 to 20 times.

Lunges

You will have noticed throughout this section of the guide that I have been providing you with simple, yet highly effective exercises that can be carried out at home. The lunge exercise, which works the thighs and bottom, is another great addition to the range of exercises that require no attendance at the gym. Lunges also fit perfectly into the role of an Army soldier simply because they concentrate on building the necessary core muscles to perform the demanding tasks of the job.

To begin with, stand with your back straight and your feet together (you may hold light hand weights if you wish to add some intensity to the exercise).

Next, take a big step forward as illustrated in the diagram making sure you inhale as you go and landing with the heel first. Bend the front knee no more than 90° so as to avoid injury. Keep your back straight and lower the back knee as

close to the floor as possible. Your front knee should be lined up over your ankle and your back thigh should be in line with your back.

To complete the exercise, exhale and push down against your front heel, squeezing your buttocks tight as you rise back to a starting position.

Try to repeat the exercise 15 to 20 times before switching sides.

Tricep dips

Tricep dips are brilliant at building the muscles at the rear of the arm. Because the tricep muscle is a core part of upper body strength you should spend time developing it. Once again you do not have to attend a gym to work on it.

- **Step 1** – Place your hands shoulder width apart on a bench or immovable object as in the diagram.

- **Step 2** – Lower your body until your elbows are at an angle of 90°.

- **Step 3** – Push back up so your body returns to the starting position, breathing out on the way up. Ensure that your back remains close to the bench or immovable object throughout the movement.

The above exercises will allow you to improve on your upper and lower body strength which will in turn improve your chances of passing the ADSC fitness tests.

Alternative exercises

Swimming

Apart from press-ups, lateral raises and the other exercises I have provided you with, another fantastic way to improve your upper body and overall fitness is to go swimming provided you have access to a swimming pool and can swim.

If you are not a great swimmer you can start off with short distances and gradually build up your swimming strength and stamina. Breaststroke is sufficient for building good upper body strength providing you put the effort into swimming an effective number of lengths. You may wish to alternate your running programme with the odd day of swimming. If you can initially swim ten lengths of a 25-metre pool then this is a good base to start from. You will soon find that you can increase this number easily providing you carry on swimming every week. Try running to your local swimming pool if it is not too far, swimming 20 lengths of breaststroke, and then running back home. (But don't forget your stretches in between!)

This is a great way to combine your fitness activity and prevent yourself from becoming bored with your training programme.

The multi-stage fitness test or bleep test

A great way to build endurance and stamina is by training with the multi-stage fitness test or bleep test as it is otherwise called.

The multi-stage fitness test is used by sports coaches and trainers to estimate an athlete's VO$_2$ Max (maximum oxygen intake). The test is especially useful for players of sports like football, hockey or rugby. You will most certainly have to carry out the test during your initial Army basic training.

The test itself can be obtained through various websites and it is great for building your endurance and stamina levels.

Training programmes

I believe it is important to add some form of 'structure' to your training programme. Apart from keeping you focused and motivated it will also allow you to measure your results. If I was going through selection right now then I would get myself a small notebook and pencil and keep a check of my times,

distances, repetitions and exercises. I would try to improve in each area as each week passes. In order to help you add some form of structure to your training regime four sample training programmes of differing intensity follow. Before you carry out any form of exercise make sure you consult your doctor to ensure you are fit and healthy. Start off slowly and gradually increase the pace and intensity of your exercises.

You will notice that each of the exercises provided as part of the training programmes is specifically designed to increase your ability during the ADSC fitness tests.

Training programme 1

Day 1	Day 2	Day 3	Day 4	Day 5
1.5-mile run (best effort). Record and keep results	3-mile run	Swimming (500 metres)	3-mile run	Swimming (500 metres)
50 sit-ups and 50 press-ups or as many as possible	50 sit-ups and 50 press-ups or as many as possible	10-mile cycle ride	50 sit-ups and 50 press-ups or as many as possible	50 sit-ups and 50 press-ups or as many as possible
3-mile walk at a brisk pace	Pull-ups (as many as possible)	20 lunges each side and 30 star jumps	Pull-ups (as many as possible)	3-mile walk at a brisk pace

Day 6 and Day 7 = rest days

(This applies to all training programmes outlined in these pages.)

Training programme 2

Day 1	Day 2	Day 3	Day 4	Day 5
1.5-mile run (best effort). Record and keep results	Swimming (500 metres)	5-mile run	2-mile walk at a brisk pace followed by a 3-mile run	Swimming (1,000 metres)
50 sit-ups and 50 press-ups or as many as possible	10-mile cycle ride	50 sit-ups and 50 press-ups or as many as possible		50 sit-ups and 50 press-ups or as many as possible
30 squat thrusts	20 lunges each side and 30 star jumps	Pull-ups (as many as possible)	Pull-ups (as many as possible)	30 squat thrusts, 20 lunges each side and 30 star jumps

Training programme 3

Day 1	Day 2	Day 3	Day 4	Day 5
1.5-mile run (best effort). Record and keep results	5-mile run	20-mile cycle ride	5-mile run	Swimming (1,000 metres)
50 sit-ups and 50 press-ups or as many as possible	50-sit ups and 50 press-ups or as many as possible	3-mile walk at a brisk pace	50 sit-ups and 50 press-ups or as many as possible	50 sit-ups and 50 press-ups or as many as possible

(Continued)

 how2become

(Continued)

Day 1	Day 2	Day 3	Day 4	Day 5
Swimming (500 metres)	Pull-ups (as many as possible)	30 squat thrusts, 20 lunges each side and 30 star jumps	Pull-ups (as many as possible)	30 squat thrusts, 20 lunges each side and 30 star jumps

Training programme 4

Day 1	Day 2	Day 3	Day 4	Day 5
1.5-mile run (best effort). Record and keep results	Bleep test (best effort)	7-mile run	Swimming (1,000 metres)	10-mile run
50 sit-ups and 50 press-ups or as many as possible	Pull-ups (as many as possible) followed by 50 squat thrusts, 25 lunges each side and 50 star jumps	70 sit-ups and 70 press-ups or as many as possible	Pull-ups (as many as possible) followed by 50 squat thrusts, 25 lunges each side and 50 star jumps	70 sit-ups and 70 press-ups or as many as possible
Swimming (1,000 metres) followed by a 3-mile brisk walk	20-mile cycle ride	30 squat thrusts, 20 lunges each side and 30 star jumps	10-mile cycle ride	Swimming (500 metres) followed by a 3-mile brisk walk

Tips for staying with your workout

The hardest part of your training programme will be sticking with it. In this final section of your fitness guide I will provide some useful golden rules that will enable you to maintain your motivational levels in the build up to the Army Development and Selection Centre (ADSC) assessment. In order to stay with your workout for longer, try following these simple rules.

Golden rule 1: Work out often

Aim to train five times every week.

Each training session should last between 20 minutes to a maximum of an hour. The quality of training is important so don't go for heavy weights but instead go for a lighter weight with a better technique. On days when you are feeling energetic, take advantage of this opportunity and do more!

Within this guide I have deliberately provided you with a number of 'simple to perform' exercises that are targeted at the core muscle groups required to pass the Army fitness tests. In between your study sessions try carrying out these exercises at home or get yourself out on road running or cycling. Use your study 'down time' effectively and wisely.

Golden rule 2: Mix up your exercises

Your exercise programme should include some elements of cardiovascular training (running, bleep test, brisk walking, swimming and cycling), resistance training (weights or own body exercises such as press-ups and sit-ups) and, finally, flexibility (stretching). Make sure that you always warm up and warm down.

If you are a member of a gym then consider taking up a class such as Pilates. This form of exercise class will teach you how to build core training into your exercise principles,

and show you how to develop your abdominals in ways that are not possible with conventional sit-ups. A fantastic 'all round' exercise that I strongly recommend is rowing. Rowing will exercise every major muscle group in your body and is perfect for improving your stamina levels and cardiovascular fitness. It is also a great exercise for preparing for each of the strength tests that form part of the ADSC assessment.

Golden rule 3: Eat a healthy and balanced diet

It is vitally important that you eat the right fuel to give you the energy to train to your full potential. Don't fill your body with rubbish and then expect to train well. Think about what you are eating and drinking, including the quantities, and keep a record of what you are digesting. You will become stronger and fitter more quickly if you eat little amounts of nutritious foods at short intervals.

Golden rule 4: Get help

Try working with a personal trainer or someone else who is preparing for selection. They will ensure that you work hard and will help you to achieve your goals. The mere fact that they are there at your side will add an element of competition to your training sessions! A consultation with a professional nutritionist will also help you improve your eating habits and establish your individual food needs.

Golden rule 5: Fitness is for life

Working out and eating correctly are not short-term projects. They are things that should be as natural to us as brushing our teeth. Make fitness a permanent part of your life by following these tips, and you'll lead a better and more fulfilling life!

Good luck and work hard to improve your weak areas.

A FEW FINAL WORDS

You have now reached the end of this book and no doubt you will be ready to start preparing for the Army selection process. Just before you go off and start on your preparation, consider the following.

The majority of candidates who pass the Army selection process have a number of common attributes, as follows:

They believe in themselves

Regardless of what anyone tells you, you *can* pass the selection process and you can achieve high scores. Just like any job of this nature, you have to be prepared to work hard in order to be successful. Make sure you have the self-belief to pass the selection process and fill your mind with positive thoughts.

They prepare fully

Those people who achieve in life prepare fully for every eventuality and that is what you must do when you apply

to become a soldier with the British Army. Work very hard and especially concentrate on your weak areas. In this book I have spoken about deliberate and repetitive practice. Identify the areas in which you are weak on and go all out to improve them.

They persevere

Perseverance is a fantastic word. Everybody comes across obstacles or setbacks in their life, but it is what you do about those setbacks that is important. If you fail at something, then ask yourself 'why' you have failed. This will allow you to improve for next time, and if you keep improving and trying, success will eventually follow. Adopt this same method of thinking when you apply to become a soldier.

They are self-motivated

How much do you want to join the Army? Do you want it, or do you *really* want it? When you apply to join the Army you should want it more than anything in the world. Your levels of self-motivation will shine through when you walk into the AFCO and when you attend the ADSC. For the weeks and months leading up to the selection process, be as motivated as possible and always keep your fitness levels up as this will serve to increase your levels of motivation.

Work hard, stay focused and be what you want . . .

Richard McMunn

INDEX

how2become